LOUISIANA'S ITALIANS, FOOD, RECIPES, & FOLKWAYS

LOUISIANA'S ITALIANS, FOOD, RECIPES, & FOLKWAYS

Nancy Tregre Wilson

PELICAN PUBLISHING COMPANY
GRETNA 2007

First printing, October 2005
Second printing, November 2007

Library of Congress Cataloging-in-Publication Data

Wilson, Nancy, 1942-
Louisiana's Italians, food, recipes, and folkways / by Nancy Wilson.
p. cm.
ISBN-13: 978-1-58980-318-3 (pbk. : alk. Paper)
1. Cookery, Italian. 2. Cookery, American—Louisiana style. I. Title.
TX723.W59 2005
641.5945—dc22
2005014345

Front cover photograph: Rosa Passarella Culotta and daughter Angelina dressed in Sunday finery.
Back cover photograph: The Trentacosta family with their mud oven in Brittany, Louisiana.

Printed in the United States of America

Published by Pelican Publishing Company, Inc.
1000 Burmaster Street, Gretna, Louisiana 70053

Dedication

To my mother-in-law, Angelina Culotta Wilson. I treasure the many hours I spent with her as she shared stories of her Italian heritage.

To Toni Albers, my niece. I promised that if she recovered from Hodgkin's disease, publishing this book would be my thanksgiving to St. Joseph and our Lord.

To my four children, Angela, Tregg, Charlena, and Nanette. In spite of being French, German, and Scotch-Irish, in their minds, they are Italian first. The first manuscript for this book was written in 1972. Tregg was five months old and Angela, five, when I started dragging them around researching Italian traditions and collecting recipes.

To Gina Arrigo-Wilson, my daughter-in-law, who, too, treasures her Italian heritage.

To my son-in-law, James Thornton, whose encouragement with the words, "Ms. Nancy, I think you' ve got a book there," has led me to the next writing project.

And to my husband Charles, who once described me as a "wannabe" Italian. He lets me be myself. What more can I ask for?

Wedding of Charles Carmelo Culotta and Angelina Fertitta, children of Italian immigrants, took place April 15, 1928, in Beaumont, Texas. They settled in Leesville, Louisiana, where the Culottas and Fertittas became prominent political and business people.

Contents

Acknowledgments

Thank you to all the people who spent time with me to share their special recipes and memories, who embraced my children as I visited with them and their families, and who let me bake with them in spite of the fact that I am not Italian. Some people said only Italians could make those cookies.

A great big thank you to my husband for his love and support. Who else would give up his space on the carport to his wife' s mud oven? Who else would undertake building a mud oven with no masonry or carpentry experience? He has made my dream come true.

Thanks to my uncle, Joe Songy, who is a "jack of all trades." Uncle Joe and I began talking about building a mud oven thirty years ago. His knowledge has proven invaluable.

Thanks to my beautiful, supportive children who think I am a "little nuts." In spite of that, they have always been there to help me through my many projects, whether they involve technological, culinary, or business skills. And they have to admit that my being a little nuts has given them the confidence to believe that they, too, can make their dreams come true.

Introduction

To Be Italian in a Place Other Than Italy

Although there were relatively few Italians throughout Louisiana at the time of the Civil War, there existed in New Orleans a small, established colony as early as 1850. At that time Italians were mainly employed in the import business. The vast amount of Mediterranean goods, mainly citrus, provided employment for many. Approximately 97 percent of the Italian population had

The four Passarella sisters came to the United States from Cefalu at the turn of the century. Story has it that Rosa Passarella gave birth to her son Joe on the boat coming over from Italy.

migrated from Sicily. Many had come from Palermo and Messina following the trade route to New Orleans. By 1890 there were over eleven thousand Italians residing in Louisiana's sugar parishes (Scarpaci 1975, 165-83). Here they found employment distributing, unloading, and peddling fruit in New Orleans and the surrounding parishes (Magnaghi 1986, 41-45). Up until 1980, Cannoto, "the fruit man," could be seen peddling fruits and vegetables from his truck on the streets of St. Charles, Jefferson, and Orleans Parishes. Sunseri sold live chickens on Jefferson Highway, and the local cobbler was, invariably, an Italian who had learned his craft in the "old country."

To be Italian in America meant that individuals had to sacrifice to become a part of the economic growth of society. Many Italians who came to America through the efforts of the Louisiana Immigration League worked on the plantations just long enough to accumulate savings. Money was then sent to other family members for passage to the "land of opportunity." Many times the whole family worked, including the elderly and children as young as five years. The Italians lived frugally, growing their own food and saving for an opportunity to move up the economic strata. Industriousness was encouraged. Long before education became important, the development of various marketable skills was necessary. Many an uncle or father taught his skills to family members to be farmers, butchers, bakers, cobblers, or masons. Their hard work and strength of character served them well as they began to move from laborer to tenant to landowner to businessman and finally into the professions (Baiamonte 1972, 34-39).

Lydia Randazzo, in a paper for the Southeast Historical Association, writes that to be American meant to have a chance for a better life than what was possible in Italy. As agriculturists in Italy, these people faced poverty and a precarious future. There also existed a grave concern about population in relation to income from the land. In America, a forty-two-acre farm could be purchased at five dollars per acre. It is not a wonder that they chose America for resettlement.

The fishermen came, too. My husband's grandfather, Salvatore Culotta was known for his courage on the water. In the Italian community, he was so well known that two generations later his grandson, Monsignor Salvatore Culotta, was recognized as a possible relative of the infamous "Crazy Salvatore" by a neighborhood barber.

A Close Community

As the word spread of opportunity in America, extended families began to settle in Louisiana. Because of the availability of land

Rosa Passarella, widow of Salvatore Culotta, and her daughter, Angelina, dressed in Sunday finery.

and the success of the Italians with strawberry farming, Tangipahoa Parish became a favored area (Baiamonte 1971, 97-101). Other settlements could be found in Plaquemines, Jefferson, St. Mary, Assumption, Ascension, and West Baton Rouge Parishes. But because of the large population of Italians in Tangipahoa, especially in the city of Independence, this area became known as "Little Italy."

The Italians' self-imposed isolation in Tangipahoa Parish provided an opportunity for them to be Italian in a place other than Italy. They practiced the simple rituals of day-to-day living such as bread, wine, and pasta making. They also established more elaborate traditions. Hence, in Louisiana there are Italian marching clubs, Italian festivals, St. Joseph altars, St. Rosalie parades, and a variety of Italian benevolent societies. Through these customs, the early Italians gradually redefined themselves as a community in America. They reestablished the close family ties of the Italian villages with family, fellow villagers, and co-nationals; thus, a familiar setting was created, counterbalancing the foreign aspects of American life (Baiamonte 1972, 14-91).

Providing social opportunities as well as familiar commodities for the Italian community, many Italian merchants, such as the late Calvin Christiana Sr., were founders of Italian benevolent societies reminiscent of those of the old country. These societies, often named for a favorite saint, served fraternal and welfare functions. They provided health benefits and burial costs for the families of their members and others in need in the community. In addition, they sponsored social functions such as anniversary celebrations and religious observances. Many of these societies reflected Old World emphasis on town and regional traditions and loyalties. As a result of their pride in an Italian figure, the celebration of Columbus Day was a favorite (Scarpaci 1975, 165-83).

Two of the early societies were the Societa Italiana de Mutua Beneficenza in Nuova Orleans and Tiro-al-Bersaglio. Each society was formed for the purpose of providing mutual assistance for it members as well as widows and orphans of deceased members. A review of the officers revealed that their occupations were varied. There was a ship builder, a hardware dealer, an importer, a grocer, a rice dealer, and a shoemaker. The names Lanata, Christina, Solari, Barelli, Brisolara, and Rivera, which can be found on early society documents, are Italian names that are still prominent in the community at large (Magnaghi 1986, 49-61).

Even in the early days, the new immigrants made their presence

A well-dressed Italian lady. Notice the crocheted collar on her dress.

known. They had come as an undereducated populace from a country where they were all but ignored. In Italy the electorate went to those who could read, write, and had a little income. This was not so in Louisiana. By 1912, Louisiana's Italians began to enter the political arena. One of these commissioners was Charles Anzalone, an Italian immigrant who had labored on a sugar plantation, raised strawberries near Independence, and organized one of the first associations in Tickfaw. Although he had only a third-grade education, he was elected one of Independence's five town aldermen in July 1914 (Baiamonte 1972, 210-13).

According to the official proceedings of the Independence Town Council, Charles Anzalone was the first Italian elected to political office in Tangipahoa Parish, where he began a very impressive public career. During his six years as alderman, he supported progressive legislation, which provided for the town's first waterworks and fire fighting equipment, better streets, and sanitation. One of the most unusual ordinances offered by the Italian Catholic immigrant was a "blue law" that prohibited the sale of beer—but not wine!—on Sunday. Eventually, other members of Italian communities in the area were to follow and become prominent political figures on the Louisiana political scene. That legacy can be seen today with Nick Congemi, the police chief of Kenner, and Phil Capitano, Kenner's mayor (Baiamonte 1972, 210-13).

Despite blending into the culture of their new homeland, Italians would not lose their Old World traditions in the American mélange. Family relationships reigned over every aspect of life. Religious observances were important in providing hope in the struggle to become part of the society of their adopted country. The fabric of Italian culture continued, first because of close family ties and second because of the tendency of the immigrants to settle near one another. By grouping themselves in certain areas of the state, they were able to maintain control of their families. Though they welcomed the opportunities offered by their new homeland and received others into their homes with food, wine, and warmth, they were careful to protect their children from the influences of the wider society. No matter how poor, there were tablecloths on the tables and wine and bread at every meal. Pride in appearance was important. My friend Cheryl Cannizzaro Faust told me this story. As a child, she often wore shorts and skated the block in her neighborhood, her hair flying in the wind and her knees dirty from falls. The Cannizzaro family all lived on the same block near what is now Earhart Boulevard. If her grandmother

Nona saw her in this condition she would call out to her, "Chera, you comma here. You looka like a ragamuffin." Nona would then proceed to brush her granddaughter's hair, braid the long black hair into tight plaits, and "clean her up."

Another common practice among many in the Italian community was gambling. Gambling provided respite from the harsh realities of life but proved to be a downfall for some. My husband's uncle, Joe Culotta, left the area for Las Vegas back in the forties. The family had lost track of him. He had become a "professional gambler." When I met Uncle Joe, he was "down and out." Fascinated by his colorful past, I asked him to teach me to how to deal cards. With a flick of the wrist he could pull cards from any part of the deck; that I never learned. He assured me that he was an honest gambler. Once I brought him a pair of dice, having heard that he could roll them up and down the scale. He padded the table with several layers of newspaper, covered it with a cloth, then proceeded to throw the dice in a sequence . . . 2, 4, 6, 8, 10, 12 then 12, 10, 8, 6, 4, 2. Apparently gaming was in his family's blood for several of his Fertitta relatives became very successful in the gaming and restaurant industry in Nevada and Texas.

Living the Religion

Whatever other associations may be connected with Italians, perhaps most important to this community is their expression of their religion. According to Fr. Neutsie Culotta, festivals honoring saints abound in Italy. Here in America, St. Joseph and St. Rosalie are honored with parades and feasts sponsored by Italian American organizations. The feast of St. Lucy, a patron of those who suffer eye diseases, is now celebrated annually on December 13 by the eating of cuccia (coo-cheea). It is said that when Lucy, a beautiful young maiden with sparkling eyes, rejected a heathen nobleman, her eyes were gouged out and she was tortured to death. It is believed that she went blind on December 13, the day on which she is now remembered.

St. Joseph's Day and St. Rosalie's Day, formerly village celebrations in the old country, now enjoy the support of organized groups of Italians in Louisiana today. September 14, the feast of St. Rosalie, is a day of sacrifice, devotion, and festivities. In Kenner, the annual St. Rosalie Parade is a prayerful march of devoted Christians, not necessarily Catholic. The parade ends with a feast of Italian foods at Our Lady of Perpetual Help Church recreation building. Of course, crusty Italian bread, meatballs and spaghetti, biscotti, olive salad, and wine are served.

A St. Joseph's altar featuring unusual Italian pastries.

Back in 1972, I spoke with eighty-eight-year-old Theresa Gennusa of New Orleans about the feast of St. Rosalie. She remembered the celebrations of her childhood in Harvey and Kenner, known then as Carson City, as very emotional. People walked barefoot, crying, praying, and making penances, promises, and donations to the church in the name of St. Rosalie. The early celebrations included a parade, speeches, food, and fireworks. It was not unusual for people to give money, jewelry, even wedding rings should a favor have been granted by the saint.

The following is an account from *Gumbo Ya Ya* of an exchange between two Italians marching in a St. Rosalie parade many years ago. It illustrates the deep connection between heritage and religion.

> Two men argued loudly over the fact for the first time the flag of Italy was not carried. Each has an excellent, though sophistic argument, one stating that "the Catholic Church is really Italian, since Rome is in Italy, and the Pope is Italian, and he is in Rome, and most everybody in Harvey is Italian, so Harvey is Italian, and Saint Rosalia is Italian, etc., etc." What, he demanded, did Mussolini have to do with it? "Saint Peter was Italian, too," he concluded, a bit triumphantly.
>
> "You alla time want to be a damn Dago!" said the other.

> "Harvey is American, and you are American, and now Saint Rosalie is American, and Saint Peter was never no Italian. He was a Jew!"

One of the best known of all Italian feasts is St. Joseph's Day. On March 19, the day designated by the Catholic Church as the feast of St. Joseph, elaborate altars are erected in his name. The appeal of St. Joseph to so many people probably lies in the fact that he was an honest, hardworking laborer who smashed his thumb, got splinters in his fingers, and perspired just like the majority of mankind. Despite all this he was still deemed to be worthy of the Mother of God. Intricately designed Italian breads and cuccidati are cornerstones to the altars. Organizations usually sponsor altars in order to maintain the traditions of this important devotional day in their communities, and individuals usually have altars in thanksgiving for favors granted.

Those observances that began as personal and ethnic traditions have now become public symbols of Italian heritage. It bodes well for the people who came with nothing and established themselves in the fabric of a foreign community. Their hard work, faith, perseverance, and pride in accomplishment have served them well.

St. Joseph Altars...Oral Histories

With the immigration of the Sicilian Italians to the United States in the early 1890s and 1900s came the religious traditions of the old country. From the onset they continued celebrations of religious feast days as they had in Italy.

Mike Paleo of the Italian American Marching Club of New Orleans is known for his scholarly interest in Italians in America. According to his research, the celebrations of St. Joseph's Day originated during the famines of the Middle Ages. When crops failed, the Italian farmers were left with only their faith in St. Joseph. They prayed that he would intercede for them and that they might have successful crops. During the fifteenth century, when elaborate celebrations were held, the Franciscans dedicated St. Joseph's Day as a special feast day.

The story most commonly accepted as the basis for the St. Joseph altar tradition is based on St. Joseph's intercession during the famine. Mrs. Joe Bosco of Luling, Louisiana, added that this is the legend in which her husband's family believes. She said that the fava bean, which is given to each person visiting an altar, was the "lucky" bean that saved the Italians during the famines. This was the only food they had to tide them over until their first successful crop.

Another story, related by Sidney Roppollo of Baton Rouge, is that one day Jesus, Mary, and Joseph were journeying through the countryside when they met a farmer. Upon recognizing them, the farmer invited the Holy Family into his home. The family's meager supply of food was set out for the visitors. Thereafter, the farmers and townspeople prayed to St. Joseph when seeking favors and protection for their families.

Still another version of the origin of the altar is that a group of exiled Italians were set adrift in a small boat. In despair, they prayed to St. Joseph that their lives be spared and promised that, if spared, they would honor him the rest of their lives. At last finding themselves on the shore of an island, they erected an altar using branches, palmetto leaves, and red flowers in thanksgiving. Today, red St. Joseph lilies are often found on the altars as a symbol of that gratitude.

In Dedication

The spirit of devotion and thanksgiving in which the first St. Joseph altars were offered is still obvious in the dedication of the altars. Theresa (Noto) Millet of Baton Rouge said that the custom of altars was brought by her family from the "old country." Altars in the Noto family were usually promised for the safe return of loved ones from war and recovery from illnesses.

Mrs. A. J. Terracina of Opelousas, Louisiana, writes that the Bona Fidem Fraternity and Auxillary had an altar for many years. All the members of the organization helped in the preparation of the food. The altar was offered each year for peace in the world.

Kay Mortillaro of New Orleans told me that she has never offered an altar but that each year she helped with the baking and cooking for one or more altars. Many of these altars were pledged for recovery from illnesses. Mrs. Mortillaro helped with the altar of one lady who wanted to recover from her illness so that she might live to dedicate another altar.

Mrs. Frances (Roppollo) Thomassie always enjoyed the work that went into the prepar-ations for altars. Although she did not have one every year, she was always willing to help others. Her mother's crocheted bedspread was often used as a tablecloth for altars. If Mrs. Thomassie was not using it, she offered it to a friend. The amazing thing about the bedspread was that Mrs. Roppollo was able to duplicate the design of another bedspread by counting the various stitches in the pattern then crocheting her own.

The Gros altar in Chalmette during the forties.

One of the most touching stories was that of Mrs. Joe Zito of Baton Rouge. When Mr. Zito became ill with bleeding ulcers, the doctors feared that he would not live. Upon learning the news, Mrs. Zito and her son, Joe, left the hospital and drove to church to pray. She prayed at all the altars, "Please St. Josie, don't take my husband now. I make you altars the rest of his life." Upon returning to the hospital, her husband's condition was much improved. The doctor walked up to her and said, "I know you've been praying. Your husband is much better." Fourteen years later her husband died of a heart attack, but Mrs. Zito continued to make an altar for "St. Josie" each year.

As much as Mrs. Joe Zito loved St. Joseph, sometimes she lost patience with him. One year, she had worked so hard that her feet began to swell. At twelve o'clock that night, she sat down in the living room and propped up her feet. When her daughter came in from a date, she heard her mother saying, "St. Joseph, if you want me to finish this altar, you'll have to make me feel better. I can't do anything else unless you make me feel better." The next morning

Mrs. Zito was feeling much better and was able to finish her altar, which she had pledged in thanksgiving for her husband's recovery from a heart attack.

Mrs. Albert Veuch Culmone of Baton Rouge related that during the depression her father lost his job. Determined to find employment, he walked to Standard Oil. On the way, he promised St. Joseph that if he were employed that day he would have an altar each year of the rest of his life. Each year for fifty years the Veuch family has had an altar. His daughter, Mrs. Culmone, continued to make altars after her father's death.

A Celebration of Thanksgiving

Though the altars originated as a way to express gratitude, they have also become part of a large community celebration and feast, for next to their love of God and patron saints, especially St. Joseph, Italians are known for their love of food. Here, many families have St. Joseph Day dinners with pasta Milanese, pasta with red, meatless sweet gravy topped with breadcrumbs. In Italy, St. Joseph is honored by the eating of fritelli (rice fritters) or small, round loaves of bread. Sicilians, in particular those of Palermo, have been known to have elaborate banquets to celebrate the figure that devout Italians look upon as the patron saint of the universal church, carpenters, cart makers, unwed mothers, orphans, and families. They often beseech him to intercede for them so that God will grant special favors. This prayerful plea is never taken lightly and often the person asking the favor makes an offering of an altar. In Europe, the St. Joseph celebrations are church community celebrations. They are not necessarily held in thanksgiving for a favor granted.

In Sicilian villages, mass at the local church begins the celebration. Next is the procession through the village to the *banchetto,* or feast. A ceramic statue of St. Joseph is carried on the shoulders of the young men of the village. An orphan boy is chosen to depict the Bambino Gesua, a young girl the role of Mary, and an old carpenter as Joseph. They mount mules and parade through the streets, followed by the barefoot villagers who have had favors granted by St. Joseph. Crowds cheer them as they lead the way to the feast prepared by the townspeople. Villagers rush out to hand "Jesus," "Mary," and "Joseph" gifts of chickens, eggs, money, sweets, and bread. When they reach the banchetto, the priest blesses the food, and the meal begins with the shouting of "Viva San Giuseppe." Food is passed around the table, family style, when all are seated.

Intermittently, shouts of "Viva San Giuseppe" are heard as people partake of fresh fennel, black olives, thick soups, pasta, omelets, fish, fresh fruit, sweets, bread, oranges, and pastries in memory of the day. The merriment, dancing, and celebration conclude and the people return to the somber days of Lent.

Local celebrations of St. Joseph's feast day maintain many of the traditions established in the Old World. Mr. Roppollo related that many years ago the Italians in Baton Rouge held an elaborate pageant preceding the St. Joseph feast. Three people depicting Jesus, Mary, and Joseph on a journey were attacked by twenty-four "gangsters," or robbers, riding horses. As the first man lifted his sword to kill Jesus, two angels appeared and shouted, "Hail!" The twenty-four gangsters fell to the ground. Then one by one they arose and followed the "Holy Family" to the house where the feast was to be held.

According to Angelina Cangelosi Crawford, it is the custom in the Kenner, Louisiana, area for an elderly man to represent Joseph, a sixteen-year-old-girl to take the part of Mary, and a two-year-old-boy to take the role of Jesus. Little girls clothed in white and wearing crowns of gold leaves or stars are the angels. Other children are sometimes included to represent special patron saints of the person giving the altar.

Although today many families bear the expense of the altars themselves, in the old days the custom was that the person who promised the altar must humble himself and beg for contributions for the feast. Today, friends, relatives, and merchants, especially Italian grocers, hearing of plans for an altar often offer contributions of candles, food, flowers, and money.

Mrs. Frank Poretto of Houma remembered the altars in New Orleans that she and her husband visited with his aunt, Jenny Poretto. The New Orleanians "advertised" their altars by placing greenery outside the door or by tying a donkey at the front of the house to indicate that an altar had been erected and the public was welcome. She said olive branches, Japanese plum branches, or palmetto leaves were used. Notices were also put in the personal column of the local newspaper inviting the public to visit.

Preparing the Altar

The ritual of the feast, size of the altars, and variety of food found on St. Joseph altars vary according to local customs. Each family has its own rules for arranging the altar. All agree it must be as beautiful as possible and food must be plentiful. Great effort is made to arrange flowers, fruits, candles, holy pictures, statues, and food as artistically as possible. The arrangement of accessories is usually symmetrical. Bundles of uncooked pasta, packages of beans and rice, and fresh finnochi are often found on the altars. In years past, late governor Earl K. Long's picture could be found among the pictures of patron saints. Sometimes side altars are made to honor other saints. In addition to the St. Joseph altar, some families have a side altar to St. Patrick in which everything from the cloths on the tables to the cakes are shades of green.

Everyone agrees that the altar should always be placed in a very prominent location in the home. Most often it is placed in the dining room against a straight wall or in a corner. Long tables extend the structure into the living room. The altar base may be anywhere from five to seven feet tall. It usually has from three to five steps above the tables that form side and front extensions to the main altar.

The men in the Joe Bosco family of Luling, Louisiana, built a five-tiered structure and later surprised the ladies of the family by assisting in the decorating. Mrs. Joe Bosco, who made her first altar in the 1970s, was not Italian. She was born Lillian Champagne, a little French lady who married into an Italian family. As plans for her altar were being made, each person remembered something important to the event. Aunt Rosie Migliore of Good Hope, Louisiana, remembered that a large St. Joseph candle must be placed in a bucket of sand alongside the altar. Aunt "Phine" (Josephine Tamburello) of St. Rose, Louisiana, said that they had to have Yellow Rice. Though Aunt Phine didn't know how to make it, Aunt Ester Bosco had a recipe for it. Aunt Corrine Bosco filled in the details for serving the saints. Aunt Sarah Migliore insisted that there must be two of each vegetable and fruit. It is traditional to make an effort to obtain scarce and out-of-season produce.

Altars in the New Orleans area tend to be very elaborate. This is an account of an altar from *Gumbo Ya Ya:*

> Mrs. Messina sat heavily in a chair . . . and mopped at her flushed face with a damp ball of a handkerchief. From her perspiring state and the tantalizing aroma drifting from the rear of the house it was simple to deduce she had just finished preparing the food for the altar at the opposite end of the room. . . . "You like my alter, eh? I have five hundred different kinds of food."

Mrs. Messina was probably exaggerating but all the families take pride in the variety of foods and the huge quantities prepared for the feast. In 1973, Mrs. Culmone said she cooked sixty-five pounds of spaghetti. Family and friends prepare foods weeks in advance in anticipation of the altar, and visitors to the altars sometimes number in the hundreds.

Today, on the eve of St. Joseph's Day, a priest comes to the home to bless the altar, which is bedecked with foods of all types. Many people sit up during the night to pay homage to their patron saint. Others come visit to get a glimpse of the altar before the serving begins on the next day. Pastry and wine are sometimes served at this time. On the morning of the feast day, family and friends attend mass and return home to complete preparations for the hundreds of visitors who come either to manifest their devotion to St. Joseph or just out of curiosity.

Anna Monica of Garyville, Louisiana, remembered that at noon on St. Joseph's Day her father, Frank Monica, would take his shotgun outside and fire into the air to signify the time to serve the people and begin the celebration. This tradition continues in the Plaquemine area. Hiram Hebert had the honor of opening the feast to friends in this manner at his wife's first altar in 1974. Of course, today this tradition has been discontinued in nonrural areas.

It is customary in other areas to begin the celebration with the seating of the children at a special table. Other pageants begin with the children knocking at the door and welcomed into the home by the hostess. They are then seated, and the priest blesses the food if this was not done the previous day. At noon, children depicting Jesus, Joseph, and Mary are seated at a special table set with the family's best china, linen, and crystal. It is customary in some areas to have as many as six or eight additional "saints." Angelina Cangelosi Crawford of Kenner, Louisiana, writes that the Holy Family and "angels" take their places at the table with Joseph sitting at the head, facing the altar. Next to him is a staff made of bread. Mary sits at the right of St. Joseph and Jesus sits at this left on a white satin cushion in the place of honor. Those representing angels and saints fill in the remaining places.

The official opening of the feast to the public begins after the saints have eaten an appetizer of orange slices. The saints must taste each of the foods on the altar. According to Margaret "Boots" Blanchard of Plaquemine, Louisiana, they are served pasta Milanese with boiled eggs and bread, then fish, followed by vegetables and pastries. No altar is complete without the standard Milanese sauce for the pasta. It is made with fennel and sardines rather than the usual meatballs or sausage and served with mudrica in place of cheese. Mudrica, also called St. Joseph sawdust, is a mixture of fine, toasted breadcrumbs and sugar. The beverage served to the saints includes water or tea for children or wine or tea for adults. Typically, the public is served food prepared especially for the feast day while the food on the altar is given to the poor.

A fish holds a place of honor in the display and on the menu. It

The Wilson altar in 1972. In keeping with the tradition that this pilgrimage would bring blessings, Nancy Wilson, daughter Angela, and baby Tregg visited nine altars in 1974.

is important for two reasons. During the time of Christ, the fish was a symbol of Christianity. The Greek word for fish, *icthus,* is an acrostic meaning "Jesus Christ, Son of God, and Savior." It is also important because the celebration is during the Lenten season, so in the old tradition it is a meatless feast.

Frances Thomassie of Baton Rouge always baked her fish in a "standing" position propping it up with sumptuous stuffing of shrimp and rice. Theresa (Noto) Millet said that the fish is the centerpiece to the altar and that it is always lavishly garnished with lemon slices, carrot curls, and parsley. The fish is always baked with the head intact, and an olive is used in place of the eye. The fish contributed to the Bosco family's altar in 1973 was so large that it had to be baked in three pieces and reassembled for the altar.

Anna Misuraca said that her mother, Mrs. Joe Zito, believed that nothing is too good, too difficult to make, or too hard to get for St. Joseph. Making certain that no altar in the neighborhood would be without St. Joseph bread, Mrs. Vernon Varnell of Baum's Bakery in Plaquemine, Louisiana, said that in 1973 they made breads in the shapes of wreaths (a symbol for Mary), crowns, crosses, and braids, each adorned with a small ball of dough to symbolize the infant Jesus. They used fifteen hundred pounds of flour. Traditionally, each "saint" is given a bread. Others are often promised to friends and family members.

Aunt Mary (Culotta) Morrell of Beaumont, Texas, had an advantage over most when it came time to bake bread for her St. Joseph altar. Uncle Neutsie Morrell was the local Italian baker. They baked bread in at least three different shapes. The bigger and the fancier the bread, the better seems to be the theme. Some types of bread found on altars were as large as two feet in diameter. Uncle Neutsie, in the old Italian tradition, baked miniature loaves to give to those who came to visit the altar.

There is a legend, popular among the Italians, that a piece of St. Joseph bread thrown to the wind during a storm will calm the weather. A story often told is that a pious old Italian lady, probably from Morgan City, broke a portion of the bread into four pieces and placed a piece in each corner of the house during a storm. At once, the house ceased trembling. Immediately, everyone in the house fell to their knees and gave thanks to God who had protected them through St. Joseph.

Though more closely associated with breads, St. Joseph must surely have had a sweet tooth; a visit to any altar will confirm it. Tables and tables are laden with traditional Italian pastries as well as cakes of every color, size and shape. Lamb-shaped cakes are often found on the main altar alongside the cheese-filled cannoli and cuccidati. Theresa Gennusa of New Orleans, whose family had altars for over thirty-five years, said you can't have an altar without the cuccidati (fig cakes). They are made in the form of a crucifix, a chalice, and a monstrance. The pastry dough is very elaborately and intricately carved to represent the ornate details of these and other altar accessories. Mrs. Zito also made these cakes in the form of eagles and fish.

Mrs. Tony Pigno, a Michelle of Independence, said that her Italian mother always made German cookies for their altars from a recipe that has been in her family for years. The pastries are baked weeks in advance of the celebration. Georgette Cornelius (Corneglio) of Baton Rouge said that a favorite storage and hiding place for the pastries is a large garbage can. Cookies stored in plastic bags and stored in the cans will keep very well. It is important to hide the can from the family if you expect to have cookies for your altar.

Cookies and breads are not the only important additions to the St. Joseph altars. Wine is also a traditional component of the celebration. Muscatel and Marsala were two of the popular wines that were often served before the availability of Italian wines in the United States. The Italians of South Louisiana often made local substitutions, serving their own strawberry, orange, fig, blackberry, and peach wines. These take the place of the sweet and dry Marsalas. Some families serve Manischewitz. Other families, defying tradition, serve beer at their altars.

Italians could not settle in south Louisiana and not have a little of the Creole rub off on them. Red beans, crawfish bisque, boiled seafood, and stuffed crabs are often served alongside the pasta, stuffed artichokes, favas, and froscia.

These intricately prepared Louisiana dishes are always complemented by displays of flowers, vegetables, and fresh fruit. Fances (Roppollo) Thomassie told me this story about Sidney, one of the nine Roppollo children. The children, Sam, Nick, Sidney, Delia, Josephine, James, Frances, Rose, and Nina, all grew up speaking Italian. One day Sidney was sent out to buy bananas. As he walked up to the fruit stands, the wife of the proprietor turned to her husband and said in Italian, "Sell him the soft ones. They are no good." To her surprise, Sidney turned to her and answered in Italian, "I don't want the soft ones." The owners were so embarrassed they apologized and gave him the bananas. Though these two individuals were dishonest, most Italian merchants prided themselves on their integrity. An expression of the agricultural and merchant background of many of the altar's visitors, the fruits, vegetables, and flowers exhibited on the altar may be as beautiful as the surrounding wealth of baked delicacies.

After marveling at the great display, visitors to altars in south Louisiana will certainly receive a bag of goodies. It will surely include a fava bean, which has been oven dried, a small loaf or a piece of St. Joseph bread, and pastries. The bean is for good luck, the bread is said to bring prosperity, and the pastries are to enjoy the next day or on the way home if the visitor is not fasting during Lent. The Boscos of Luling also like to include a St. Joseph prayer card in their "Italian doggie bags."

An Undying Tradition

The St. Joseph's Day celebration is dear to the hearts of the Italians and they take it personally if anyone or anything should dare interfere with their devotional. In 1940, St. Joseph's Day happened to be during Holy Week. Archbishop Joseph Francis

Rummel of New Orleans asked that the celebrations be held in April. According to a story in *Gumbo Ya Ya*, some irate Italians refused, asserting that St. Joseph would not like his day changed. Mrs. Corneglio of New Orleans had her altar on the nineteenth of March as usual. "Ain't it a shame to change St. Joseph's Day?" she demanded. "It's not right to do a thing like that. The whole world, she gone crazy!" She sighed disgustedly. "How'd you like somebody to change your birthday?" Other Italians took advantage of the decree and had two celebrations. No one quibbled over that.

Shirley Dauzat of Baton Rouge tells of an aunt who had an altar in June, immediately after the saint granted her favor. One year, Mrs. Zito had three altars at different times throughout the year.

Anna Monica of Garyville, Louisiana, said that as a child she felt overwhelmed by the physical size of the altar that her parents had each year. When I last spoke with her she said that the reality is that the work that goes into altar preparation is overwhelming. Perhaps that is part of the reason that today many organizations sponsor altars.

Mrs. Sam Cherry of Thibodaux, Louisiana, wrote that the Italian American clubs of Thibodaux and Houma, Louisiana, had elaborate, sixteen-foot St. Joseph altars for many years. The custom was revived in the sixties in an effort to preserve some of the traditions of the old country. Now in this twenty-first century, we again are seeing a revival of St. Joseph altars.

Some families, including the Dittas of New Orleans, the Culottas and Fertittas of Leesville, and the Lamendolas of Shreveport, often celebrate St. Joseph's Day with family dinners, as do many families in other parts of the country, especially in the northeast.

Unfailing Petition To St. Joseph

This prayer to St. Joseph was given out to visitors attending the Bosco altar in Luling, Louisiana, many years ago.

> Holy St. Joseph, Spouse of Mary, be mindful of me, pray for me, watch over me. Guardian of the paradise of the new Adam, provide for my temporal wants. Faithful guardian of the most precious of all treasures, I beseech thee to bring this matter to a happy end if it be for the glory of God and for the good of my soul. Amen.

The newspaper notice of the altar generally reads as follows:

> All parishioners are cordially invited to attend the Bosco family St. Joseph altar at the home of Mr. and Mrs. Rodney Bosco. It

will be open 7:00 p.m. Saturday, March 18 and all day Sunday. A traditional dinner will be served to those attending on Sunday.

St. Lucy

(La Festa di Santa Lucia)

To Italians festivals are not just a time of celebration for the sake of merrymaking but a very sincere devotion. Festivals are held for patron saints throughout the year in Italy. The best-known ones are the feast of St. Lucy, patron of those who suffer eye diseases; the feast of St. Agatha, patron saint of nursing mothers and those who suffer diseases of the breasts; the feast of St. Joseph, patron of the family; and the festival of the Sicilian cast, or the feast of St. Alfio.

Not all of the Italian Catholic festivals survived the trip to America, but there are many remnants of these festivities in the form of "food traditions." One such food tradition is connected to the story of St. Lucy. During a famine, the Italians invoked the help of St. Lucy. While they were praying, a ship of grain arrived, thus saving the people from starvation. Hence, the tradition of eating cuccia on December 13, the saint's feast day, began.

Cuccia

On the feast of St. Lucy, cuccia is eaten as a breakfast cereal, a dessert, or a snack.

1 lb. wheat kernels, whole or cracked
2½ qt. water
2 tsp. salt

Wash wheat kernels in cold water then drain. Cover with water and soak several hours or overnight. Drain. Place in a large pot and cover with warm water. Add salt and bring to a boil. Cover and simmer for 1½ to 2 hours or until kernels are tender. Serve hot or cold.

Variations

For a breakfast cereal, heat cuccia. Add butter, syrup, or sugar and milk.

For a dessert, serve cold with cream, sugar, and cinnamon.

For a vegetable, heat and season with olive oil, black pepper, salt, and parsley.

Cooking with a Mud Oven

Mama's Italian Bread

Crusty homemade bread was literally the "staff of life" for many Italians new to this country. A favorite supper in the Roppolo family was a sandwich made of thick slices of Italian bread, olives, raw onion, oil, and a little vinegar. Frances Roppollo Thomassie said, "We were poor and that's practically what we lived on."

Aunt Lena (Fertitta) Culotta attributed her grandmother's good teeth to the eating of that hard day-old Italian bread all of her life. She had her first tooth extracted at 94 years of age and died at 96. When I expressed amazement at this she reminded me, "Well, you know all Italians have good teeth!"

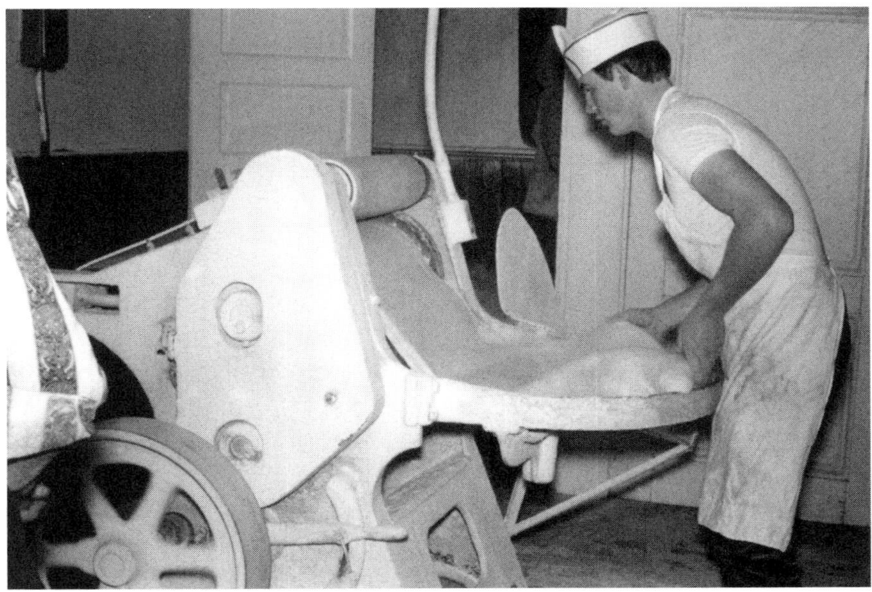

Commercial baking was one of the many crafts the Italians brought with them to this country, and the Baum's Bakery in Plaquemine is a testament to ingenuity of the Italian immigrants.

Mrs. Hiram Hebert (right) had an altar in thanksgiving for her son's recovery from a grave illness.

In 1969, Joseph and Rose Trentacosta of Brittany, Louisiana, determined to have "bread like mother used to make," built an old-fashioned Italian oven in their back yard. Their dome-shaped oven was built with the assistance of relatives and Father Dispensa, former pastor of St. Theresa Catholic Church and a native of Italy. Brother-in-law Leon Ippolito took the lead in design and construction. Rose used an old family recipe to bake bread, which is an important part of the menu in annual family gatherings. "One cooking of bread from our oven furnished enough for the annual get-together of the sixty-four members of the Ippolito-Trentacosta family," said Joe. On a weekly basis, the clay and brick structure was used to provide both friends and relatives with bread "like Mama used to make."

Mrs. Joe Zito remembered building her own "mud and brick igloo" oven. She said that it was good for other things besides baking bread. Once when her husband's boss came to her home and she didn't feel presentable, she stuck her head in the unheated oven to keep from having to greet him.

Mud ovens were not the only way to bake bread. Many years ago Mrs. Zito, Mrs. Johnny Michelle, Mrs. Frank Michelle, Frances

Roppollo Thomassie, Beth Hebert of Plaquemine, Virginia Simoneaux of Baton Rouge, and from twenty to thirty other "little Italian ladies" would show up at Baum's Bakery in Plaquemine to bake bread for altars in Baton Rouge, Plaquemine, and the surrounding areas. Vernon Varnell would open his bakery for one day one weekend prior to St. Joseph's Day for the ladies in the community. He would go to the bakery as early as three o'clock in the morning and work with his "ladies" until seven o'clock at night. One year in the early 1970s, thirteen hundred pounds of flour were used in making the "straight dough" for the St. Joseph's Bread. He said that one year a "little Italian lady" visiting from Italy was among the group. She couldn't speak a word of English but could she shape those loaves, some of which weighed as much as eight pounds!

First You Build the Oven . . .

My husband said that if he can build this oven, then anyone can build it. I took a little liberty with design to insure success for the amateur mason and to lower the cost. For example, mixing the clay, sand, and cement is much cheaper than buying a premixed product. Too, I offer tips that we discovered when assembling our own oven. Of great significance is the mud form. The mud form, packed mud around which the oven is built, is important to the integrity of the oven's shape; do not try to build this oven without a form. My husband also was concerned about bridging the gap at the top of the "igloo" so I offer the foolproof solution of using a clay planter saucer to give support and maintain shape.

These directions are for an oven with a 42-inch diameter and an inside height of about 31 inches. The outside height will be approximately 35 inches. The door height should be about 66 percent of the height of the inside of the oven. The oven can be made larger or smaller by changing the size of the circles of brick.

48 8-inch by 16-inch by 4-inch cinder blocks
80 8-inch by 16-inch by 8-inch cinder blocks
2 3-foot by 5-foot concrete boards
2 tubes of heat resistant caulking
4 6-foot by 6-foot by 1-inch boards
70 firebricks
175 "old" or solid bricks
3 yards burlap

2 50-lb. bags low-temperature potter's clay (food grade)
5 50-lb. bags fine sand
1 50-lb. bag Portland cement
1 bag vermiculite
2 10 "dry quart" bags vermiculite
1 12-inch terra-cotta planter saucer
1 20-inch by 14-inch iron door or make a "plug" door (see instructions below)
1 vent with damper
4 wheelbarrows of dirt
45 feet plastic wrap
12 daily newspapers to make a layer about 12 pages thick
1 metal doorframe, fabricated from "angle" iron (optional)
1 thermometer that measures temperatures up to 1000 degrees (optional)

Tools

carpenter's level
electric saw with mortar blade

Mortar mix: Mix 2 parts sand to 1 part clay and 8 percent Portland cement.

Mortar-insulation mix: Mix 2 parts vermiculite to the basic mortar mix.

Plug Door: Build a 4-inch-deep open wooden box, the interior of which should be 20 inches by 14 inches or the size of the door opening. Fill with clay or mortar and bricks. Place a 10-inch-long piece of a wooden two-by-four on the exterior of the box. Attach the wooden piece to the center of the box, making sure that one of the 4-inch sides is flush with the bottom of the frame. This construction will serve as a handle and provide support for the door so that it stays in place while the oven is in use.

Alternative to vent with damper: Use a whole brick to create a space for an opening in the structure. Wrap the brick in several layers of newspaper then plastic wrap. Put in place at the back of the oven in the eighth layer of bricks. When the mortar is completely dry, remove the brick from the structure. The opening will serve as an air vent. To keep cinders from flying into the air when the oven is in use, fashion a fine-screen plug to use while fire is burning.

Assembling the Oven

The foundation of this oven will provide a 15-inch ledge on which to work. The working height will be approximately 36 inches.

Step 1

In an area approximately 6 feet square, layer the 8-inch by 16-inch by 4-inch cinder blocks to make the first layer of the oven's foundation. Lay these cinder blocks so that they make 5 foundation pillars, each measuring 23 inches square. There should be one pillar on each corner and one in the middle of the square.

Step 2

Construct a tray using 4 6-inch by 6-inch boards and 2 concrete boards to make the bottom of the tray. Use 2½-inch screws to put the frame for the tray together. This tray will be set on the pillars that make the foundation. Place the tray on the cinder-block foundation.

Step 3

Fill the tray with 4 inches of fine sand. Level the sand.

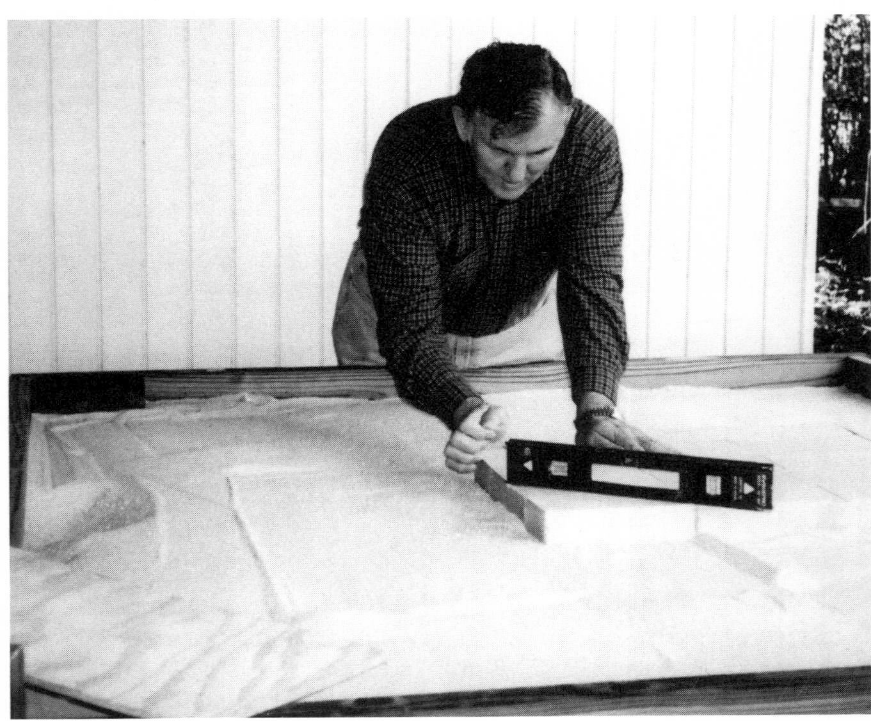

Step 4

Place the firebricks in the sand in the area on which you will construct your oven. Fill in around the firebricks with "old" bricks (solid bricks). No mortar needed.

Draw a 42-inch diameter circle on the firebrick surface using chalk or a lead pencil.

Mark off a 14-inch area to designate the width of the door.

Step 5

Place 2 layers of brick and mortar on the outer edges of the circle. These 2 brick layers should be of the same size.

Line the area of the circle with a piece of heavy plastic, letting the sides reach the 2nd level of bricks. Fill the circle of bricks with dirt, packing it to the height and shape of the finished oven. Cover the mound of dirt with wet newspapers. Shape the newspapers to the dirt form.

Step 6

Make a doorframe using scrap lumber to safeguard the space for the oven door while you build up the brick levels. Work around the doorframe when you lay the bricks. Remove the frame after oven is complete.

Step 7

Lay bricks in 9 concentric circles, offsetting each by at least 1 inch to make each circle smaller than the previous circle. Follow the shape of the dirt form. Cut the bricks in half using the mortar blade on your electric saw. Use half-bricks if necessary to maintain the integrity of your circles of bricks.

Step 8

Place the vent or make the vent (see "Alternative to vent with damper") in the 9th layer of bricks. It should be placed at the back or side near the back of the oven.

Step 9

Place another layer of bricks and mortar. You should now have a circular opening in the top of your oven approximately 10 inches in diameter. Mortar the 12-inch terra-cotta planter saucer over the last layer of bricks to cap the oven. Let oven dry for several days before putting the 2 insulation layers in place.

Step 10

Add vermiculite to the mortar mix using 2 cubic feet per layer of mortar. Smooth a 2-inch layer of mortar/vermiculite mix over the brick structure. Let dry. Cover with wet burlap. Mortar over the burlap to make another 2-inch layer of insulation over the oven. Let mortar dry thoroughly. Dig as much of the dirt out of your oven as you can. Remove the last of the dirt by pulling the plastic liner out. Clean the oven floor with a damp mop.

Place the "plug" or iron door into the structure and adjust the fit with additional mortar. Let dry several days before lighting the first fire.

Remove the vent plug. Make a fire in the oven using newspaper and kindling. Add 2 small logs to the fire and bring the temperature slowly to 750 degrees. Maintain the heat by feeding the fire. It will take approximately 3 to 4 hours to reach 750 degrees. Open the door to reduce the heat to cooking or baking temperature.

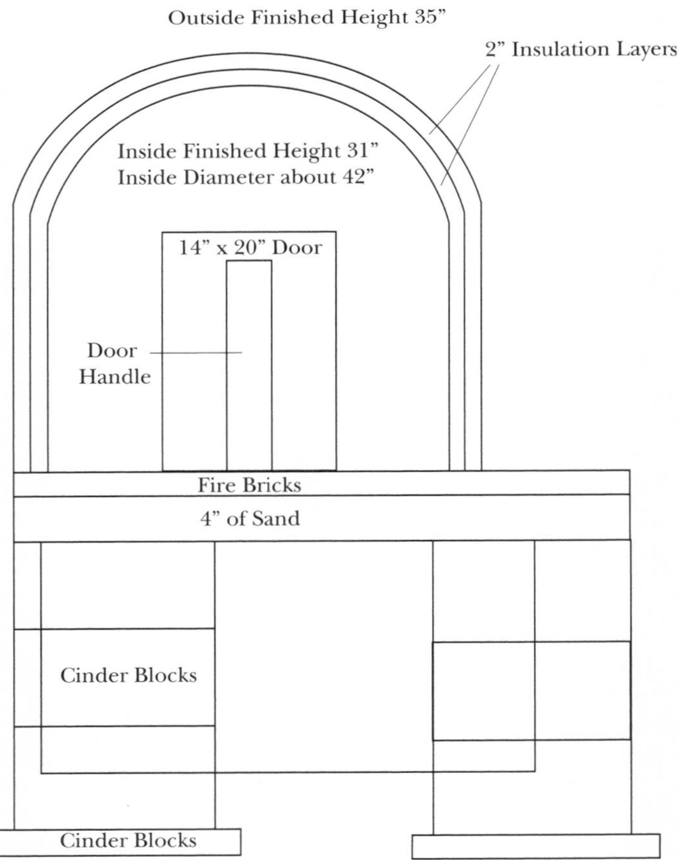

Mud oven at the Rural Life Museum in Baton Rouge.

Using the Oven for Baking

The following recipes as well as your favorite soups and stews can be cooked in the mud oven. In addition, any slow cooker recipe works well in this oven. Each of the recipes in this section may also be cooked in conventional oven at the temperatures specified.

1. One hour before baking time, light a fire in the oven, using wood logs and small scraps of lumber or small branches. Close the door.
2. In about 3 to 4 hours, the inside of the oven should be white-hot. Remove the door or plug long enough to bring the oven temperature down to the desired temperature.
3. Using a long-handled metal rake, remove the remains of the fire from the oven. Rake coals into a large can of water placed near the door opening. Hot air from the oven will singe your eyebrows and hair if you are not careful. Close the damper. Clean the floor of the oven with a wet mop.

4. Test oven temperature by using a thermometer or place a small twisted piece of paper in the oven. If it burns, the oven is too hot. If it simply turns brown, the oven temperature is around 400 degrees.

5. Use a wooden or metal palette to place food in the oven. Close the door and bake or cook according to directions in recipe.

Mama's Italian Bread

(Pane)

True Italian bread is very close textured, hard, and chewy. It is made from special hard-wheat flour, which is not found on grocery shelves. This recipe makes a type of bread that is "Italian" and very delectable but with a softer texture than the breads usually found on the altars.

1 cup lukewarm milk or water
1 package yeast
1 tbsp. sugar
3 cups all-purpose flour or bread flour
1 egg white
1 tbsp. water

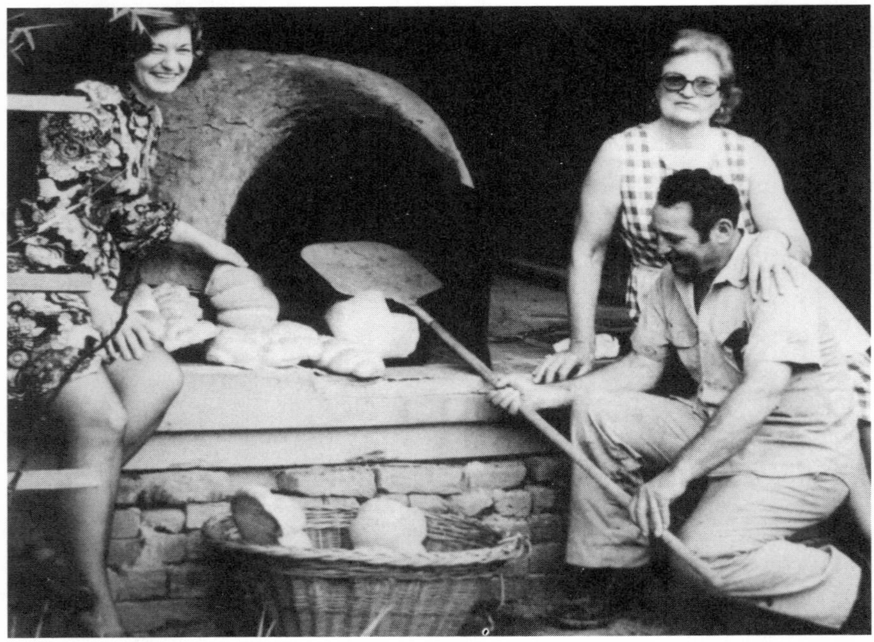

The Trentacostas wanted to make bread like "Mama used to make." They built this oven in their backyard in Brittany, Louisiana.

Dissolve yeast in lukewarm milk or water. Let it stand for 5 minutes. Add next 3 ingredients and stir well. Add flour and mix well. Let the dough rest 10 minutes. Knead well. Let rise. Punch the risen dough down. Let dough rise again then divide into 2 loaves. Shape into crowns or loaves. Place on cookie sheets sprinkled with corn meal. Brush with a mixture of 1 egg white and 1 tablespoon of water. Let rise until doubled in size.

Bake at 425 degrees or approximately 10 minutes in the mud oven. Mist with water and continue baking 35 minutes or until browned. Most loaves take about 60 minutes to bake. Makes 2 loaves.

Uncle Neutsie's Italian Bread

Angelina Culotta Wilson sent this recipe, which her brother-in-law, Neutsie made. This is the bread Aunt Mary (Culotta) Morel serves with her St. Joseph's Day feast. It is also the same bread her husband, Uncle Neutsie, made in the bakery in Beaumont, Texas, a half century ago. The bread is made into many different shapes for the St. Joseph altars. Among them are the St. Joseph staff, hearts, palms, animals, carpenter tools, and wreaths with special symbols made of dough to indicate whether it's Jesus, Mary, or Joseph bread. Blessed bread from the altar is always given to each of the children participating in the pageant.

The amount of liquid needed in the recipe will vary depending on the moisture in the air and the type of flour used. Hard-wheat bread flour will require more liquid than low-protein flour.

2 lb. yeast
12 pt. lukewarm water
12 oz. salt
12 oz. sugar
12 oz. shortening
42 lb. (12 qt.) bread flour

Dissolve yeast in lukewarm water. Add salt, sugar, and shortening. Mix well. Add flour and knead by machine (commercial mixer) for 10 minutes. Let rise for 20 minutes. Punch down and shape into loaves. Let rise until double. Bake at 450 degrees for 20 minutes. Makes 40 1-pound loaves.

Chef Angela Wilson's Ciabatta

My daughter, Angela, developed this recipe for a James Beard dinner at the James Beard Foundation House in New York City. This is an old-fashioned, chewy bread. Great served with Njoi olive oil.

1 cup and 2 tbsp. lukewarm water
8 tsp. yeast
4 cups all-purpose flour
2 tsp. yeast
9 cups flour
3 cups water
1 cup milk
5 tsp. salt
2 oz. olive oil

Mix the first 2 ingredients together in a large plastic bowl. Let set overnight. This is called the "starter." Add remaining ingredients except oil and mix well. Do not overknead dough. This will be a wet dough. Knead dough, mixing in olive oil. Place in a large bowl and let rise until it doubles in size. Flour work surface. Trying not to lose the air in the dough, divide into 4 15-inch by 6-inch rectangles. Carefully move to 4 baking sheets dusted with flour. Let rise 45 minutes in a warm place. Mist with water. Bake in a 400-degree oven for 45 minutes to an hour until nicely browned. Makes 4 large loaves.

Artichoke Bread

1 recipe pizza dough
1 16-oz. can artichokes
1/4 cup grated Parmesan cheese
4 oz. grated mozzarella or Provolone cheese
1 egg
2 tbsp. water

Divide dough in two pieces and roll each piece into a rectangular shape. Chop artichokes. Place artichokes and cheeses on one side of each piece of dough. Fold the other side of the dough over and seal edges. Brush with mixture of egg and water. Bake at 400 degrees in oven for about 10 minutes. Serve hot or cold. Makes 6 servings.

Homemade Butter

Dell Sporer said that when she was a child, she and her siblings would ride a streetcar to West End in New Orleans to visit her grandmother. They would also visit with an old Italian lady who made bread in a mud oven and made her own butter. Dell said that the bread and butter were like nothing she had ever eaten. At her house, butter was colored lard and later margarine in a bag with a "colored bead." She remembers squeezing the bag of margarine until the bead would burst to release the color. So, if you want the glorious butter that Dell remembers from her childhood visits to the West End, first you'll have to get a cow.

1 qt. cream
1/8 tsp. salt

Place cream in mixing bowl. Beat on high until fat separates from the water and the butter makes a lump in the bowl. Drain off water then beat in salt. Place in a small covered dish and refrigerate. Makes about 1 cup of butter.

Faci de Vaca

I can't remember who gave me this recipe, but it bakes quickly and I love it. Could this "Vaca" refer to the explorer Cabeza de Vaca? Perhaps his appearance was as wrinkly as that of this bread.

1 lb. bread or pizza dough
2 tbsp. Kalamata olives
1 small red onion, thinly sliced
3 tbsp. olive oil
Salt and freshly ground black pepper to taste

Flatten dough into a 1/2-inch-thick circle. Let rise in a warm place for 20 minutes. Press olives and onions into the top of the dough. Drizzle with olive oil, salt, and pepper. Bake at 400 degrees until lightly browned. Makes 4 servings.

Easter Egg Bread

(*Pane Uovo di Pasqua*)

Elaborate celebrations for Easter are traditional with Louisiana's Sicilians. Devout Italians that they are, they attend daily mass during the Lenten Holy Week before Easter. On Easter Sunday the family congregates for an elaborate get-together. Food plays an important part in the festivities. Using the Christian symbol for life and the Resurrection of Christ, the egg, they make Easter baskets, or *Buba Cul Uovo,* for Easter breakfast. Brightly colored eggs are baked in dough, which is shaped in the form of baskets, bunnies, chickens, and wreaths, or *corona di nove*. The Lawrence Gambino family of Waggaman, Louisiana, include the Easter Breads in their St. Joseph altar. According to Mrs. Gambino, the altar should be adorned with St. Joseph lilies (red lilies), and the predominant color in decorating should be red (St. Joseph's color.)

Easter Egg Baskets

This sweet dough is more like cookie dough than bread dough.

1 tsp. salt
5 tsp. double-acting baking powder
1 cup sugar
3 cups flour
3 eggs
¼ to ½ cup milk
½ tsp. vanilla
½ tsp. lemon juice
1 cup butter
8 to 10 eggs, raw and colored red

Sift dry ingredients together. Beat together eggs, milk, vanilla, and lemon juice. Using your fingers or a pastry blender, cut the butter into the dry ingredients as you would for biscuits. Make a well in the center of the dry ingredients and add the liquid mixture. Mix well. On a floured board kneed the dough until it is no longer sticky. Shape dough around each egg to form a "basket." Place a strip of dough over the egg to look like a basket handle. Bake at 375 degrees for about 20 minutes or until dough is lightly browned. Cool.

Frosting
1 box powdered sugar
1/4 cup water, approximately
1/4 cup shortening
1 1/2 tsp. almond flavoring
Silver and multicolored nonpareils

Beat powdered sugar, water, shortening, and almond flavoring until light and fluffy. Frost baskets and decorate with nonpareils and frosting. Makes 8 to 10 individual baskets.

Easter Egg Bread

Here is the yeast-bread version of the Easter Egg Bread.

2 1/4 to 3 cups all-purpose flour
1/4 cup sugar
1 tsp. salt
1 7- or 10-gram package active dry yeast
2/3 cup milk
3 tbsp. margarine
2 eggs
1/2 cup mixed candied fruit (optional)
1/4 cup chopped blanched almonds
1/2 tsp. anise flavoring or 1/4 tsp. anise oil
5 eggs, raw and colored
Powdered sugar frosting
Colored sprinkles

In a large bowl, mix 2 1/4 cups flour, sugar, salt, and undissolved yeast. Combine milk and margarine in a saucepan. Heat until liquid is warmed and margarine is melted. Gradually add this liquid and 2 eggs to dry ingredients. Beat well. Add additional flour until dough is soft. Turn out on floured board and knead until smooth and elastic. Grease the top of the bread and place it in a bowl in a warm place to rise until it doubles in size. Punch down the risen dough. Shape into 2 long ropes and twist them into a wreath. Place colored eggs in wreath. Let rise for approximately 1 hour or until doubled in size. Bake at 350 degrees for approximately 35 minutes. Cool. Frost and decorate with colored sprinkles. Makes 1 large bread wreath.

Crostini

12 slices white bread
3 oz. butter
2 tbsp. flour
1 cup milk
2 tbsp. grated Parmesan cheese, extra
Salt
Pepper
1/4 cup finely diced mushrooms
2 tsp. anchovy paste
2 tbsp. Parmesan cheese
1/3 cup canned rolled fillets of anchovies
6 olives
1/4 red pepper

Cut 2 2-inch circles from each slice of bread. Melt 2 oz. butter in pan, brush both sides of bread with butter, and place on oven tray. Bake in a 325-degree oven 10 minutes or until golden brown. Cool. Melt extra butter in pan, add flour, and cook 1 minute. Add milk, stir over moderate heat until mixture boils and thickens, remove from heat, add cheese, salt, pepper, and finely diced mushrooms; mix well. Add anchovy paste and stir through the mixture. Spread spoonfuls of mixture over bread and top with extra Parmesan cheese. Place anchovies in center of some bread circles. Halve olives and discard pits. Cut pepper into thin strips. Decorate remaining circles with olives and pepper. Bake in hot oven for 5 minutes. Makes about 24 servings.

Muffuletta

1 round Italian bread, split
1/4 lb. mortadella
1/4 lb. Genoa salami
1/4 lb. ham
4 slices provolone cheese
1/2 cup olive salad, Boscoli or Mosca's brands or make your own (see Index)
2 tbsp. olive oil

Layer all meats and cheese on one piece of bread. Spread olive salad on meats and drizzle with olive oil. Cut in 4 pieces. Makes 4 servings.

Crisp Crust Pizza

This pizza can be prepared and frozen for later cooking, or the crust can be made, precooked, and frozen for later use.

1 pkg. yeast
1/2 tsp. sugar
1/2 cup lukewarm water
1 1/2 cups flour
1/4 tsp. salt
2 tbsp. oil

Place yeast and sugar in water. Let stand for five minutes. Sift flour and salt in a bowl, then add oil and yeast mixture. Mix to make a firm dough. Knead for 10 minutes. Place dough in a lightly oiled bowl to rise. Cover and let stand in a warm place for 30 minutes or until dough is double in bulk. Punch dough down and knead into a smooth ball. Roll to a 10-inch circle.

Pizza Sauce
2 tsp. oil
1 small onion, chopped
1 clove garlic, chopped
2 cups whole tomatoes
1 tbsp. tomato paste
1/2 tsp. oregano
1/2 tsp. basil
1 tsp. sugar
1/4 tsp. salt
1/4 tsp. black pepper

Toppings
4 oz. mozzarella cheese
2 tbsp. Parmesan cheese
2 oz. anchovies
1/3 cup black olives
3 large mushrooms, sliced

Brown onion in hot oil. Add garlic and cook for one minute. Add tomatoes and remaining ingredients. Bring to a boil and simmer for 15 minutes. Cool. Spread on pizza. Combine cheeses and sprinkle over pizza. Top with anchovies, olives, and sliced mushrooms or your choice of topping. Bake in 400-degree oven for about 20 minutes. Makes 4 servings.

Pizza Dough

1 package yeast
1 to 1¼ cups lukewarm water
4 cups bread flour
1 tbsp. extra virgin olive oil

Place yeast in lukewarm water. Let stand for about 5 minutes. Add remaining ingredients and mix well. Knead until dough is smooth and elastic. Let dough rest for 30 minutes. You might want to break off a piece, pat it into a circle, and try shaping the dough into a large circle by throwing the dough into the air, catching it on your knuckles to stretch it. Pat or roll the dough out and bake at 400 degrees for 10 minutes. Smear tomato gravy on the pizza and add your favorite toppings. Sprinkle with any Italian seasoning blend. Place in oven and bake until cheese is hot and bubbly. Makes 2 servings.

Pasta Carbonnaro

This dish comes from northern Italy. It is a family favorite and easy to prepare.

1 lb. bacon, fried crisp; reserve grease
⅓ cup chopped onion
2 cloves garlic, minced
¼ tsp. nutmeg
¼ tsp. black pepper
2 eggs, slightly beaten
1½ cups whipping cream or half and half cream
⅔ cup grated Parmesan cheese
1 lb. package spinach or regular fettuccini, boiled

Fry bacon until crisp. Drain bacon but reserve grease. Sauté onions in 2 tablespoons bacon grease. Add garlic and sauté another 5 minutes. Add remaining ingredients, including bacon, and mix well. Place in a 9-inch by 13-inch casserole dish. Bake at 350 degrees about 20 minutes. Makes 8 servings.

Almost Mama Leoni's Bolognese Sauce

Mama Leoni's is a famous New York restaurant noted for authentic Italian food. Though the restaurant's recipe is delicious, to suit my family's taste, I leave out the liver, which was part of the original recipe.

4 slices bacon, diced
1/4 cup butter
1/3 cup olive oil
1 large onion, chopped
2 cloves garlic, mashed
1/2 tsp. fresh chopped rosemary
1/2 tsp. bay leaf powder or 1 bay leaf
1/2 lb. "sweet" Italian sausage
1/2 lb. ground beef
6 tbsp. white wine
1 28-oz can crushed tomatoes
2 medium plum tomatoes, chopped
1/8 tsp. nutmeg
1 cup hot water

In a 3-quart Dutch oven, fry bacon until crisp. Remove bacon and add butter, olive oil, and onions. Sauté for 10 minutes then add garlic, rosemary, and bay leaf. Continue cooking for 10 minutes. Remove sausage meat from casing. Add meat and cook until sausage is brown. Add remaining ingredients to Dutch oven. Cover and place in a 350-degree oven for approximately 35 minutes. Serve sauce over your favorite pasta. Makes 6 to 8 servings.

Vicky's Great Artichoke Stuffing

My friend Vicky (Maggio) Woodall prepared this casserole for a Christmas party and received rave reviews. It is easier than stuffing artichokes and just as good.

2 14-oz. cans artichoke hearts with liquid
4 cups Italian-style breadcrumbs
1 cup Parmesan cheese
1/4 tsp. garlic powder, or to taste
3/4 cup olive oil
Provolone cheese (optional)

Chop artichoke hearts. Combine remaining ingredients, including water from artichokes. Place in a 2-quart casserole dish. Top with provolone cheese, if desired. Bake at 325 degrees for about 30 minutes. Makes 8 servings.

Can't-Be-Beat Green Bean Casserole

Rich and yummy, this casserole has been a family favorite for years. We always serve this casserole for holidays, and I always get recipe requests for this casserole when I prepare it for a potluck supper. I love it when my friends, not knowing that I prepared it, ask me if I've tried the wonderful green bean casserole!

1/2 cup chopped onion
1/2 cup butter or margarine
1 can cream of mushroom soup
8 oz. Colby or sharp cheddar cheese, grated
30 Ritz crackers, crushed
2 cans French-style green beans, drained

Sauté onions in butter or margarine then add mushroom soup. Grate cheese. Put crackers in food processor to make crumbs. Mix cracker crumbs with grated cheese. In an 8-inch by 8-inch casserole dish, layer soup mixture with green beans and cracker mix, ending with cracker mix as the top layer. Bake at 350 degrees for 30 minutes. Makes 6 servings.

Shrimp and Eggplant Casserole

We always had eggplants in the garden during the summer, and the casserole made from those eggplants was a favorite. Most times Mom would scoop the pulp from the eggplants and fill the shells with this dressing.

4 large eggplants
1 cup onion, finely chopped
2 cloves garlic, minced
2 ribs celery, minced
1/4 cup and 2 tbsp. butter
1/4 cup parsley, chopped
1/3 tsp. powdered thyme
1 tsp. powdered bay leaf
1 1/2 cup shrimp, peeled, chopped, and precooked or 1 lb. crabmeat
1 tsp. salt
1/4 tsp. black pepper
5 slices bread, soaked in water then squeezed
1/2 cup plain breadcrumbs

Split eggplants in half lengthwise. Boil in salted water until tender then scoop out pulp. Reserve 4 shells. Sauté onion, garlic, and celery in 1/4 cup butter until tender and translucent. Add remaining ingredients except breadcrumbs. Mix well, breaking up lumps of bread. Pile filling into shells. Melt 2 tbsp. butter in skillet. Add breadcrumbs. Toast the breadcrumbs then sprinkle over filling. Bake at 350 degrees for 30 minutes. Serve hot. Makes 4 servings.

Eggplant/Zucchini Casserole

2 large zucchini or eggplants, sliced
2 large onions, sliced
4 large tomatoes, sliced
Salt, pepper, and dried basil to taste
2 cups tomato or V-8 juice
2 cups mozzarella cheese

Butter large casserole dishes. Layer vegetables, sprinkling each layer with salt, pepper, and basil. Pour juice over vegetables and top with cheese. Cover and bake at 350 degrees for 45 minutes. Makes 8 servings.

Pork and Cabbage Casserole

2 lb. pork chops
3/4 cup onion, chopped
1/4 cup parsley, chopped
4 cups cabbage, shredded
1 tsp. salt
1/8 tsp. pepper
1/8 tsp. allspice
2 apples, chopped (optional)

Combine all ingredients except apples. Cover and place in oven. Bake on low at 325 degrees for 5 to 6 hours. Add apple slices and cook 30 minutes longer or serve raw slices of apple with casserole. Makes 8 servings.

Artichoke and Oyster Soup

This soup is very much like the one served at the restaurant Corinne Dunbar's many years ago.

3 tbsp. butter or olive oil
1 pt. oysters, drained and chopped
2 qt. boiling water
1 package Mam Papaul's Gumbo with Roux mix
2 16-oz. cans artichoke hearts
1/4 cup sherry
1/4 tsp. powdered bay leaf
1/4 tsp. powdered thyme
Salt, pepper, and hot sauce to taste

Melt butter. Sauté oysters then add boiling water. Whisk in Mam Papaul's Gumbo with Roux mix and add remaining ingredients. Simmer at 325 degrees for 25 minutes. Serve with Melba Toast. Makes 6 servings.

Make-It-and-Forget-It Vegetable-Beef Soup

Let your mud oven do the work and watching for you.

1 3-lb. chuck roast or 3 beef shanks
3 tbsp. oil
5 beef bouillon cubes
3 qt. water
1 6-oz. can tomato sauce
1 large onion, chopped
1 cup chopped celery
3 cups frozen mixed vegetables
2 tsp. salt
1/4 tsp. black pepper
3 potatoes, peeled and diced
4 oz. angel hair spaghetti
4 cabbage leaves, shredded

Cut roast into 1-inch cubes or leave shanks whole. Add next 9 ingredients. Bring to a boil. Place uncovered in mud oven and bake at 300 degrees. Simmer for about 4 hours then add potatoes and pasta. Continue cooking until potatoes and pasta are tender. Add cabbage, cover, and let stand 10 minutes before serving. Makes 12 servings.

Toky Toky Taco Soup

This is a great soup that cooks well in the Italian mud oven. Mexicans of the Southwest use outdoor clay ovens even today for making dishes that requires long, slow cooking.

1 lb. lean ground beef
3/4 cup chopped onion
1 28-oz. can chopped tomatoes
1 14-oz. can red beans or pinto beans
1 17-oz. can corn
1 8-oz. can tomato sauce
2 qt. water
1 tsp. salt
1 package taco seasoning mix
1 cup grated Monterey Jack or Colby cheese
Taco or corn chips

Brown beef and onions in a 4-quart Dutch oven. Combine all ingredients except cheese and taco chips. Place pot in oven with lid askew. Cook at 250 degrees for 3 hours. Serve with cheese and chips. Makes 8 servings.

Meat Broth

Use residual oven heat to make broth for use with a later meal.

1 large hen, cut into 10 pieces, or
3 lb. beef or pork bones with some meat
1 onion, quartered
4 garlic cloves, crushed
4 celery ribs
1 1/2 tsp. salt
1 bell pepper, chopped (optional)
2 carrots, chopped
2 qt. water

Place all ingredients in a 4-quart Dutch oven. Cover and bake at 350 degrees for 4 to 6 hours. Drain. Makes approximately 2 quarts broth. Use meat in salads or hash.

Easy Chili

This chili can be left unattended while the family cook tends to other tasks. Turn the dish into Italian Cincinnati Chili by adding a ½ teaspoon of cinnamon along with the chili powder.

1 lb. lean ground beef
1 large onion
2 cloves garlic, minced
1 tsp. salt
1 tbsp. chili powder
1 tsp. cumin
2 tsp. Worcestershire sauce
1 16-oz. can kidney beans
1 14½-oz. can crushed tomatoes
1 6-oz. can tomato paste
2 cups grated cheddar cheese

Brown meat. Add onions and garlic. Cook until onions are translucent then add remaining ingredients except cheese. Cover and cook at 400 degrees for 3 hours or 7 to 8 hours at 325 degrees. Serve with cheese. Makes 8 servings.

Chinese Citrus Chicken

Chicken has been a common meal to many rural Louisiana families because nearly every family that lived in Louisiana's rural areas had a chicken house. Despite the prevalence of this dish, most people do not know how to properly cook chicken. Many overcook chicken then complain that it is dry. For a juicy, tender meal, bake seasoned chicken breast at 350 degrees for 45 minutes.

1 3-lb. chicken
1 cup orange juice
⅓ cup chili sauce
2 tbsp. soy sauce
1 tbsp. molasses or cane syrup
2 tsp. garlic powder
½ bell pepper, chopped
1 13⅓-oz. can mandarin oranges
or 1 14-oz. can pineapple chunks

Wash and dry chicken. Place in one layer in baking dish. Combine remaining ingredients and pour over chicken. Cover and cook on low in mud or conventional oven at 350 degrees for 4 hours or until chicken is cooked throughout. Serve over rice. Makes 4 to 6 servings.

Boston-Baked Beans

This is a great baked bean dish that can be cooked in the outdoor oven. In years past, when both men and women worked in the fields, they favored bean dishes because they could be cooked unattended. Cooked navy beans were often combined with cauliflower and broccoli in meat stocks to make inexpensive but hearty soups. Though this bean dish is not Italian, it was enjoyed by Italians. Ever hear of a baked bean sandwich? True thrift!

1 lb. bacon
1 large onion
3 garlic cloves
1 No. 10 can baked beans
½ cup brown sugar
1 cup catsup
1 tbsp. mustard

Cook bacon until crisp. Remove bacon from skillet and add onion and garlic. Cook 10 minutes. Add remaining ingredients. Cover and place in 300-degree oven until heated throughout. Makes 25 servings.

Baked Pumpkin

This is like eating candy, so sweet and delicious!

1 6-lb. cushaw or pumpkin
½ cup butter
2 cups sugar
¼ tsp. salt
1 tsp. cinnamon or pumpkin pie spice

Wash outside of pumpkin or cushaw. Do not peel. Cut into quarters then 1-inch slices. Melt butter in baking pan. Lay slices in butter, trying not to overlap slices. Mix dry ingredients and sprinkle over pumpkin. Toss to coat with butter and sugar mixture. Place in oven at 350 degrees for 2 hours or until sugar has turned to a thick syrup and pumpkin is candied. Serve with ice cream or use as a preserve on toast. Makes 12 servings.

Baked Pumpkin in the Shell

Here is a dish that came from over the ocean, originating with the Italian love of various types of squash. Pumpkin, zucchini, "cagoozza" (a long squash often cooked in red gravy), and striated "crooked neck" squash were part of the diet of the Italian farming community. Many Italians were "truck" farmers who sold the best of their crops and fed their families what which might not have been acceptable in commercial trade. Despite these hardships, Italians enjoyed this recipe, which is easy to prepare and a joy to serve.

1 pumpkin, 5 to 6 lb.
6 eggs
2 cups whipping cream
3/4 cup brown sugar
1/2 tsp. cinnamon
1/4 tsp. nutmeg
1/4 tsp. ground ginger
4 tbsp. melted butter
Pinch of salt

Cut a circle out of the top of the pumpkin as you would for a jack-o-lantern. Remove seeds and debris. Mix remaining ingredients and place in pumpkin. Cover pumpkin with lid and place in a baking pan. Bake at 375 degrees for approximately 2 hours until custard is set. Serve from the pumpkin for an interesting presentation. Scrape the meat of the pumpkin and serve with the custard.

Baked Sweet Potatoes

Sweet potatoes, as many as desired

Wash sweet potatoes. Place aluminum foil on the floor of the oven and put potatoes on the foil. Close the oven door. Bake at 350 degrees until potatoes are soft.

Homemade Wines and Drinks

These drinks are made the old-fashioned way, with natural fermentation of the fruit. Today, more sophisticated methods and information are available from brew shops and the internet.

Anisette

Anise, or fennel, is a favorite seasoning of Italians. Fresh fennel, known as *finochini,* is used as a vegetable. Seeds and oil are used for seasoning sausage, cookies, cakes, and, of course, liquor. Italian anisette is available throughout Sicily and is often served after dinner.

1 1/4 cup sugar
1 1/2 cup distilled water
1/2 tsp. anise oil
1 qt. vodka

Mix sugar, water, anise oil, and vodka in a pot or crock. Stir until sugar is dissolved. Let stand one month or longer before using. Color with red or green food coloring for Christmas, if desired. Makes approximately 2 quarts.

Blackberry Cooler

A cool, light alternative to wine.

1 bottle Manischewitz Blackberry Wine
2 liters lemon-lime soda
2 cups frozen blackberries
2 qt. shaved ice

Combine all ingredients. Mix and serve. Makes 2 1/2 quarts.

Blackberry Wine

Anna Vincent Misuraca of Baton Rouge says that sweet blackberry wine is often served at her family's altar. Here is a recipe, compliments of Ernest Keller Jr. of Hahnville, Louisiana, who got it from some Italian friends when he worked "across the river." He said it has been a long time since he has made the wine, and he didn't remember who gave it to him.

6 lb. blackberries
1 gal. water
2 lb. sugar

Pick and wash berries then place in a 3-gallon crock or stainless steel pot. Using your hands, mash berries. Let stand for 3 days. Strain and discard berries. Add water and sugar to blackberry juice. Cover with a clean cloth and let stand about 6 weeks. Strain into sterilized quart-sized bottles. Makes about 5 quarts.

Peach Wine

John Labate of Independence, Louisiana, said, "Come to the Little Italy celebration in May. We're just 4 miles from Tickfaw. You know where Tickfaw is." The Italian Catholics of Independence have declared Independence the "Little Italy of the South." St. Joseph's Day, which is March 19, is celebrated with parades and feasting. A statue of St. Joseph adorned with blue ribbons is carried through the streets. Donations are made to the church by pinning money onto the blue streamers. John says, "You won't find any one dollar bills pinned to St. Joseph, either!" In the spirit of that time of celebration, here is one of John's favorite wines.

1½ bushels ripe peaches
4 gal. water
13 lb. sugar

Wash peaches. Place in a large crock or pot and cover with water. Heat until peaches are soft. Transfer water and peaches to a large pot and cover with a clean cloth. Let ferment about 3 days. Place peaches in a cloth and squeeze out remaining juices. Discard seeds and pulp. Sweeten juice with sugar and let stand, covered with a clean cloth, about 3 months. Your wine is now ready to drink or be bottled. Makes about 16 quarts of wine.

Fig Wine

John Labate claims you can make wine with anything that will ferment. He even tried making watermelon wine. Figs, John says, are pretty sweet so you don't need much sugar—just 80 to 100 pounds.

30 gal. figs, washed
80 to 100 lb. sugar

Place figs in a 5-gallon barrel or pot for 2 to 3 days until fermented. Squeeze out the juices and throw out the pulp. Add sugar to the juice. Cover with a clean cloth. Let stand for 3 to 4 months, then bottle. If you find the wine a little strong, add a little water just before drinking. If you add water before bottling, it will sour. Makes 22 gallons.

Raisin Wine

The ancient Romans liked a heavy beverage. Their wine, often made of dried grapes, was diluted with water before serving. Today Italians still enjoy this homemade drink. My mother, Lelia (Faucheux) Tregre, remembers drinking raisin wine at the home of her brother-in-law, Nelson Falgoust, who lived in St. James, Louisiana.

2 qt. raisins, dark or light
2½ cups sugar
½ cup wine vinegar
1 gal. boiling water

Place all ingredients in a 15-quart pot or stainless steel container. Add water until the liquid reaches the 10-quart level. Cover with a clean cloth. Let stand for 10 days then strain and discard pulp. Place wine in 16 sterilized quart-sized bottles. Let wine settle. In the winter, wine is ready to drink 8 days after bottling; in the summer, after about 5 days. Dilute with water if is too "heavy." Makes about 8 quarts.

Strawberry Wine

From Anthony Corneglio of LaPlace comes this strawberry wine recipe. Anthony comes from Hammond, which is strawberry country, and his recipe makes a great homemade strawberry wine.

2 qt. strawberries or 1 qt. strawberry juice
3 lb. sugar
2 gal. water

Boil 2 quarts strawberries with 1 quart water for about 30 minutes. Place in cheesecloth bag and squeeze juice from berries into a large pot or crock. Add juice, sugar, and water. Cover with a clean cloth and let stand 6 months before serving or bottling. Makes 9 quarts.

Lemon Cello

Pronounced like the musical instrument, this recipe was given to me by Leah and Frank Arrigo. Lemon Cello is a wonderful liquor that can make use of the many Meyer lemons that are grown in south Louisiana; I imagine that similar citrus fruits could be substituted for a different flavor.

12 lemons
1 liter of Everclear or other pure grain alcohol
1 liter of water
2 lb. sugar

Remove zest from lemons. Soak lemon zest in alcohol for 14 days in a covered glass or stainless steel pot. Strain zest from alcohol and discard. Place water and sugar in a 4-quart pot. Stir. Heat until sugar is dissolved. Cool then add zest-flavored alcohol. Store in sterilized bottles. Refrigerate before serving. Makes 2 liters.

Italian Eggnog

Mama mia! Celebrate with thata spicy libation!

1 cup milk
1 egg
1 oz. brandy
1 oz. Liquore Galliano

Combine all ingredients in a shaker and shake like crazy! Chill in freezer for 15 minutes and serve. Makes approximately 1½ cups.

Neapolitan Refresher

Beautiful, dark-haired Rosita Passerella grew up working in the citrus groves of Palermo. Story has it that her mother worked for the local nuns, and her father was the gardener at the convent. Against her parents' wishes, Rosita spurned the attentions of a wealthy suitor for the love of her life, Salvatore Culotta, a humble fisherman from Cefalu known for his daring and courage on the water. In tribute to their courage to leave Italy for America, I offer this recipe.

4 fresh, ripe peaches, peeled and diced (or 8 canned freestone peaches, diced)
2¼ cups sugar
4 cups fresh-squeezed orange juice
⅓ cup lemon juice
¾ cup apricot brandy
6 sprigs mint leaves

Heat peaches, sugar, orange juice, and lemon juice in a sauce pan over low heat until sugar is dissolved. Add ½ cup brandy and mix. Freeze until icy. Serve in stemmed wine glasses and garnish with remaining brandy and mint leaves. Makes 6 servings.

Angelina's Company Coffee

My mother-in-law always welcomed company with a cup of coffee, not only because she enjoyed a "cuppa" but also out of pride. The coffee was always Seaport, the company that her cousins owned. Her nephew, Charles Culotta, shared this story about the company with me. He related that his grandfather and two cousins started the business in the '20s, when grandfather Charles Fertitta owned a grocery store. He bought coffee beans from a cousin in San Antonio and roasted the beans in a small room in the back of the store. Needing money for expansion, Charles and his cousin, Rose Maceo, were backed by their mothers-in-law. These ever frugal Italian ladies each had a secret stash of money hidden from their husbands. (My mother-in-law said this stash was called a "pootsa.") Each contributed $5,000 in exchange for 10 percent interest in the company. Eventually, the Lykes Steamship Company chose to serve the coffee on ship, hence the name Seaport Coffee Company.

6 tbsp. dark roast Seaport coffee
6 cups water
Canned milk and sugar to taste

Place coffee grounds in the top of a drip pot. Bring water to a boil then pour water slowly over the coffee grounds. Add more water as the water drips through the pot until all the water has been used. Serve hot with canned milk and sugar. Makes 6 servings.

Bay Leaf Tea

One of the fringe benefits of collecting information for this book was getting some really useful information. A little bay leaf tea does wonders for a colicky baby, according to my "little old Italian lady friends." The research for this book was completed right before my baby boy was born. Thank goodness!

2 bay leaves
1 cup boiling water
1 tbsp. sugar

Place bay leaves in water, cover, and let steep for 3 minutes. Remove leaves and sweeten with sugar. Serve warm to colicky baby. Makes 1 cup.

Appetizers

Angelina's Italian Spinach Dip

My Italian mother-in-law, Angelina Josephina Culotta Wilson, whose family came from Sicily, inspired this family favorite.

2 tbsp. olive oil
3 tbsp. flour
1 cup milk or half and half
1 small jar artichokes, drained and chopped; reserve liquid
1 8-oz. package frozen, chopped spinach, thawed
½ tsp. Italian seasoning blend
½ cup Parmesan cheese, grated
Salt, black pepper, and hot sauce to taste
⅛ tsp. nutmeg

Heat olive oil. Stir in flour and cook for two minutes. Whisk in milk or half and half. Cook until thick and bubbly. Mix in remaining ingredients. Using artichoke liquid, thin to desired thickness. Serve hot or cold with crackers. Makes 3½ cups.

Artichoke Balls

Dawn Faucheux, granddaughter of the Corraos and Sardegnas who fled Sicily at the turn of the century, shared this recipe for an interesting appetizer.

1 16-oz. can artichoke hearts, drained
¼ cup Parmesan or Romano cheese
1 tbsp. olive oil
1 tbsp. vinegar
½ cup Italian breadcrumbs
1 egg

Mash artichoke hearts. Mix in remaining ingredients and roll into small balls. Bake at 375 degrees for about 10 minutes. Makes 36 balls.

Sicilian Artichokes

(Carciofo alla Guida)

Tony Leonti of New Orleans sent the following artichoke recipe. It is a change from the usual stuffed artichokes. He says that artichokes prepared in this manner are popular among the Sicilians from around Messina and Catania. Displayed on a St. Joseph altar, this dish appears to be a plate of roses. For color, add cherry tomatoes, olives, or flat pepperoni and parsley.

4 artichokes
1 slice of lemon per artichoke
4 cups water
1/2 tsp. salt
2 tbsp. olive oil
2 tbsp. wine vinegar
1/8 tsp. black pepper
1/4 tsp. oregano
1/4 tsp. red pepper flakes
1 clove garlic, sliced

Remove stem from artichoke. With shears cut off each pointed barb and with a knife level the top of each artichoke. Very carefully pry center open with a tablespoon. Using a rotating movement, completely remove the fuzzy interior. Rinse the artichoke under cold water, rub exterior with a lemon slice, and squeeze the slice of lemon into the center of the artichoke. Boil artichokes until tender in water seasoned with 1/2 teaspoon of salt. Artichokes are tender if a toothpick easily penetrates the stem end. Remove from water and drain well. Place artichokes up on stem end and pour good Sicilian olive oil over all. Then sprinkle with wine vinegar, salt, and pepper. Dust all with oregano and crushed Italian red pepper. Add sliced garlic to taste. Cover artichokes with plastic wrap. Cool at room temperature. Refrigerate at least 1 day, allowing artichoke to marinate completely.

To serve, invert each artichoke over a plate, stem up. Place both thumbs on stem and insert fingers into center of artichoke. Press gently on the stem and at the same time pull outward on the body of the artichoke. Continue until artichoke is flattened on plate. It will look like a rosette. Pour marinated juices over each artichoke. Serve as a first course or as a salad. Makes 4 artichokes.

Stuffed Artichoke Appetizer

This is a traditional recipe for stuffed artichokes. It is the one that I am most familiar with and most commonly found in the Italian delis and restaurants in New Orleans. This is so easy and so good!

4 artichokes
2 qt. water
2 tbsp. olive oil
2 tsp. salt
1 lemon

Filling
3 cups Italian-style breadcrumbs
1/4 tsp. salt
1/4 tsp. black pepper
1 tbsp. garlic powder
1/2 cup Romano or Parmesan cheese, grated
1/2 cup olive oil

For each artichoke, trim leaves and cut stem so that it is flush to the bottom of the artichoke. Place artichokes in a 4-quart pot and cover with water. Add olive oil, salt, and lemon juice. Cover and bring to a boil. Reduce heat and simmer about 45 minutes until artichokes are tender. Drain artichokes, reserving liquid. While allowing artichokes to cool, mix filling ingredients. Spread leaves and stuff each leaf with a teaspoon or more of the breadcrumb filling. Place in a 6-inch-deep pot and pour reserved liquid into the pot. Add enough water so that there is approximately 2 1/2 inches of liquid in the pot. Bring to a boil, cover, reduce heat, and simmer for about 20 minutes until leaves are easily pulled from heart. You might need to replenish water during cooking in order to keep the bottom of the artichoke covered with water. When the artichoke is cooked, pull 2 rows of bottom leaves from the artichoke and place in 2 concentric circles on a round serving plate. Place the remaining artichoke in the center of the plate and garnish with lemon slices. This makes a beautiful presentation on a party table. Serve hot or cold as an appetizer. Makes 24 servings.

Stuffed Artichoke alla Monica

(*Carciofo Inbottiti Monica*)

Anna Monica says her mom's stuffed artichokes are the best there are. She remembers her Italian grandmother sitting near the steps of the back porch cleaning *carduna* (artichoke stems) in preparation for the St. Joseph altar. Here is Mrs. Frank Monica's recipe.

Artichokes, one per person
4 oz. fresh Romano cheese
2 tbsp. olive oil
Water

Remove stem from artichoke so that the bottom is flat. Loosen leaves so they will spread by hitting the artichoke against the top of sink. Slice cheese and place one slice in each open space between leaves. Dribble with olive oil. Set artichokes in a large, deep pan. Add about 1½ inches of water. Cover and steam over low heat until a leaf comes out easily when pulled. This will take anywhere from 40 minutes to an hour. Be sure to keep water in the pot while artichokes are steaming. Add more water if necessary. Delicious, hot or cold. Makes seasoning sauce for 2 artichokes.

Stuffed Artichokes alla Sicilian

This recipe was in the *New Orleans Times-Picayune* 75 years ago. It appeared in an article about the Sam Romano altar on Magazine Street.

1 artichoke
1 head (12 cloves) garlic, peeled and minced
1 cup parsley, finely chopped
½ tsp. salt
1 tsp. black pepper
1 tsp. olive oil
1 lemon, sliced
3 to 4 cups water

Cut stems off artichokes and trim ½ inch off top of leaves. Open and spread the leaves as much as possible. Wash under faucet. Turn upside down and drain 10 minutes. Mix remaining ingredients except olive oil, lemon, and water in a large bowl. Salt artichokes lightly. Spread artichoke leaves and pack stuffing between them. Pour 1 teaspoon olive oil on top of artichoke and top with lemon slice. Place artichoke upright in a pot with a tight lid. Pour 3 to 4 cups of water in pot, cover, and simmer over low heat for about 45 minutes. Add more water if necessary. When a leaf is easily removed, the artichoke is done. Season with additional lemon if desired. Split to make 2 servings.

Vegetable Pickles

Since vegetable farming is a mainstay for the livelihood of the many immigrants of the area, it is no wonder that pickled vegetables found their way to the cupboards and onto the dinner table.

1/4 head cauliflower
1 cucumber
2 carrots
6 small onions
Salted water for boiling
1 red pepper
2 1/2 cups white wine vinegar
12 black peppercorns
2 tsp. mustard seed

Cut cauliflower into small flowerets. Slice cucumber into quarters lengthwise and remove seeds. Then cut each cucumber quarter in half lengthwise and across. Scrape carrots, cut into thick slices lengthwise, then cut each slice in half across. Cook cauliflower, carrots, and onions in boiling salted water for 2 minutes. Drain. Combine drained vegetables with cucumber and pepper. Pack vegetables into sterilized jars. Combine wine vinegar with peppercorns and mustard seeds. Pour over vegetables to cover completely. Let stand at least one week before using. Makes 2 quarts.

Fried Broccoli and Cauliflower

So simple, yet so good!

1 small head cauliflower
1 small bunch broccoli
6 eggs
1/2 cup water
3 cups seasoned flour or Italian breadcrumbs
Oil for frying

Break vegetables into 2-inch-size pieces. Rinse well. Parboil for 3 minutes in boiling water. Drain and cool. Beat eggs with water and dip vegetables in egg mixture. Then drench in seasoned flour or breadcrumbs. Fry in hot oil. Drain. Makes 12 servings.

Stuffed Eggplant or Mirliton

Mrs. Michael Zuppardo of New Orleans is well known for her capabilities in the kitchen and in the 1960s was in charge of the annual altar at St. Joseph's Cathedral in New Orleans, which was sponsored by the Greater New Orleans Italian Cultural Society. She says that "the Italians" stuff vegetables very similar to the French and German people along the Mississippi River. So, here is my recipe with a few changes recommended by my Italian friends.

4 small eggplants or medium mirlitons
Water for boiling
2/3 cup onion, finely chopped
1 clove garlic, minced
1 tbsp. oil
1 cup shrimp, peeled, deveined, and chopped
4 green onions, finely chopped
1/4 cup parsley
1/4 tsp. salt
1 cup breadcrumbs
1/3 cup Parmesan cheese
1 1/2 tsp. oregano

Cut vegetables in half lengthwise. Place in pot of boiling water and cook for approximately 25 minutes. When tender, remove and discard seeds. Scoop out pulp and reserve pulp and shells. Sauté onions and garlic in oil until onions are tender. Add chopped shrimp and continue cooking until shrimp turn pink. Add vegetable pulp and remaining ingredients. Mix well. Pile into shells. Top with breadcrumbs. Bake 25 minutes at 350 degrees. Makes 8 servings.

Substitutions

Substitute Italian-style breadcrumbs for plain breadcrumbs, cheese, and oregano.

Spread Italian-style or buttered breadcrumbs rather than plain breadcrumbs over top of vegetables. To butter breadcrumbs, melt 4 tablespoons butter. Add plain or Italian-style breadcrumbs. Toast to light brown color. Sprinkle over vegetable halves. Bake.

Sicilian Caponato

In this book, I don't try to distinguish between Sicilian and Italian since it would be hard to divide 2 groups so closely related in so many ways. However, this recipe is supposed to be "authentic" Sicilian caponato.

1 eggplant
1 tbsp. salt
1/4 cup olive oil
1 medium onion, chopped
2 red bell peppers, seeded and coarsely chopped
1 rib celery
1 1/2 cups peeled tomatoes, chopped
2 tbsp. cider vinegar
1 tbsp. sugar
1 clove garlic, minced
8 black olives, sliced
1 tbsp. capers
1/2 tsp. salt
1/4 tsp. black pepper

Wash and cube eggplant. Sprinkle with salt then place in a colander and set aside for 1 hour. Rinse under cold water and pat dry. Heat oil in a large skillet. Add onion, peppers, and celery. Cook over medium heat for 5 minutes. Add eggplant and cook 5 additional minutes. Push tomatoes through a sieve to make a purée. Add tomato purée, vinegar, sugar, and garlic to the skillet. Cook 2 minutes longer. Add sliced olives and capers. Stir well. Simmer uncovered over medium heat for 15 minutes or until most of the liquid has been cooked out. Season with salt and pepper. Makes 1 quart.

Eggplant Appetizer Fertitta

This appetizer is called *capanata* or *caplatini* in the Culotta and Fertitta families. It is good served hot or cold as an antipasto or vegetable says Johnny Cornelius of Baton Rouge, whose ruddy complexion belies his Italian heritage. Originally Corneglio, Johnny's last name was changed to Cornelius by the army, reports his wife, and that's how it stayed.

3 large eggplants
1 tbsp. salt
3/4 cup olive oil
1 onion, chopped
1 No. 2 can Italian plum tomatoes, drained
1/2 cup olive, chopped
1 stalk celery, diced
1/4 lb. Italian green onions, chopped
1/4 cup capers
1 tbsp. pine nuts
1/3 cup vinegar
2 tbsp. sugar
Salt and pepper to taste

Wash but do not peel eggplants. Cut into 1-inch cubes. Sprinkle with salt and let stand in a colander for two hours. Squeeze dry with your hands. Heat oil in a saucepan and sauté eggplants on medium, turning constantly so eggplants will brown on all sides. Cook until soft then, using a slotted spoon, remove from pan and drain oil from the eggplants. Use oil to brown onion until soft. Add drained tomatoes, olives, and celery and cook slowly for about 15 minutes until celery is tender. Return eggplants to pan and add capers and pine nuts. Heat vinegar and dissolve sugar in it. Pour this mixture over eggplants. Season to taste with salt and pepper. Cover and cook over low heat for 20 minutes, stirring occasionally to prevent sticking. Put in jars. Makes 2 quarts.

Eggplant Appetizer Dauzat

Shirley Dauzat's *capanatini* is perfect for a company dinner. It is authentically Italian from the "old country."

Salt
8 eggplants, diced
3/4 cup olive oil
3 onions, chopped
4 ribs celery, diced
1 qt. tomato sauce
1 cup green salad olives
1 cup Kalamata olives
1 cup white vinegar
1/4 cup brown sugar
1/4 tsp. allspice

Salt eggplants and refrigerate overnight, then rinse with water and drain. Cook in olive oil until soft. Sauté onions and celery until transparent. Mix all ingredients and cook over low heat for 30 minutes. Makes 2 quarts, approximately 16 servings.

Eggplant Balls

Claire Paretto of Houma, Louisiana, serves these as appetizers or a side dish.

1 large eggplant
4 tbsp. olive oil
3/4 cup grated Parmesan or Romano cheese
1 medium onion, finely minced
1/4 tsp. salt
14 tsp. black pepper
1/2 cup Italian-flavored breadcrumbs
Oil for frying

Peel and slice eggplant. Sauté eggplant in olive oil until tender enough to mash. Add cheese, onion, seasonings, and enough breadcrumbs, approximately 1/2 cup, to make the mixture stick together. Shape into small balls and drop into hot oil to brown. Remove and drain on paper towel. Makes 4 servings.

Marinated Mushrooms

These are called *Funghi con Olio e Aceto* in Italian. This makes a great appetizer.

1 lb. small, fresh mushrooms
4 cups water
1 tsp. salt
3 tbsp. lemon juice
1 cup vinegar
1 bay leaf
1/4 tsp. thyme
2 green onions, finely chopped
1 1/2 cups olive oil
1 tbsp. catsup
1/4 tsp. black pepper

Boil mushrooms for 5 minutes in water, salt, and lemon juice. Drain mushrooms. In a small pot, boil vinegar, bay leaf, pepper, thyme, and green onions. Cool and add mushrooms, olive oil, and catsup. Marinate in refrigerator for a least 3 hours before serving. Makes 8 servings.

Olive Salad

If you have even a little Italian blood in your veins, then when you think of St. Joseph's Day, your mind will conjure visions of good food. Here is the olive salad recipe used by Sam Romano of New Orleans for his St. Joseph altar.

1 lb. green olives, pits removed
1 rib celery, diced
1 bunch green onions, chopped
1 bunch parsley, chopped to make 1 cup
6 cloves garlic, chopped
1/4 cup capers
1 bell pepper, chopped
1/2 tsp black pepper, freshly ground
1/2 cup vinegar
1/4 cup olive oil

Mash olives and remove seeds. Mix all ingredients together and let stand at least 1 hour before serving. Makes 1 quart.

Patty's Olive Salad

Patty Amato of Patterson makes this salad for company. It is a recipe that was handed down to her from her mother. Patty's grandfather, Louis Genovese, made shoes by hand in Italy. In 1912, he decided to come to America. He left his wife and 4 children, Theresa, Joe, Mary, and Mathilda, Patty's mother, in Italy. As soon as he was settled and had accumulated enough money, he sent for his family. Three years later he died. His wife later married her brother-in-law. In the United States, the family was in the shoe-repair business. The second marriage produced Louis, Martin, Claire, and Celia.

2 cups green olives, chopped
3/4 cup black olives, chopped
1 medium onion, chopped
1 clove garlic, mashed with pepper and salt
1/2 tsp. dried oregano
1/2 tsp. ground thyme
3/4 cup olive oil
1/3 cup lemon juice
1/4 cup capers

Mix all ingredients then refrigerate. Let salad come to room temperature before serving. Makes 3 cups.

Olive Tapanade

This tapanade is too good not to include. A simple recipe, it makes a great appetizer when served with a robust red wine.

1 cup oil-cured ripe olives, pits removed
1/2 cup extra pure virgin olive oil

Place olives and oil in blender and blend to a smooth paste. Use as a dip or serve on bruchetta as an appetizer. Makes 1 1/2 cups tapanade.

Mediterranean Fondue

10 anchovies in brine
6 cloves garlic, mashed
2 fresh fennel bulbs
1 green bell pepper
1 cucumber
1 zucchini
1 bunch radishes
1 cup cherry tomatoes
2 Belgian endives
1 artichoke, boiled
2 cups extra virgin olive oil
½ cup heavy cream

Wash anchovies under fresh running water to remove salt. Drain well on paper towels. Mash anchovies and garlic in a food processor. Wash, trim, and dry vegetables then cut in serving-size pieces. Separate endive leaves and arrange on trays. Put olive oil in fondue pot with anchovies and cream. When olive oil is hot, place vegetables on skewers and begin cooking a few at a time. Serve hot. Makes 6 servings.

Gorgonzola Fondue

Back in the '50s, fondue was the rage. Every new bride received at least one fondue pot as a gift. If not, it was sure to be one of her first purchases after the honeymoon. Fondue was an easy-to-prepare party food that was fun to eat. This recipe adds a bit of sophistication to the once-ordinary '50s cheddar and Swiss cheese fondues of yesteryear with Gorgonzola.

1 cup half and half
1 clove garlic, mashed
½ cup seafood or chicken broth
2 tbsp. cornstarch
½ lb. Gorgonzola cheese or high-fat-content blue cheese
1 cup white wine
Dash of hot sauce

Heat half and half with garlic in a saucepan. Simmer for 3 minutes. Remove and discard garlic. Bring half and half to a boil. Combine broth and cornstarch. Whisk cornstarch mixture into half and half. Stir and cook on low heat until mixture thickens. Stir in cheese, wine, and hot sauce. Continue cooking until cheese is melted then place in fondue pot. Keep on low heat to serve. Serve with cubed French bread. Makes 8 servings.

Fava Bruschetta

This dish can be served as an appetizer or serve as a light lunch. When I was in grade school, we called these beans "horse beans" because they were so big. As an adult I have learned to appreciate this bean for the many roles it can play in the diet, as well as on a St. Joseph altar.

Water to cover
1 lb. fava beans
1 onion
2 cloves garlic
1 tsp. fennel seed
Salt to taste
1 loaf densely textured bread, sliced
32 olives, sliced

Cover fava beans with water. Let soak for several hours. Change water; add onion, garlic and fennel seeds. Cook until beans are tender. Drain and reserve liquid. Add salt to taste. Puree to a coarse texture, adding cooking liquid as needed. Beans should not be soupy but of spreadable consistency. Place bread in oven to toast lightly. Spread fava spread on bread. Garnish with sliced olives. Makes 8 servings.

Ricotta Salata

This is another ricotta recipe from Frances Roppollo Thommasie of Baton Rouge.

1 junket or rennet table
2 qt. sweet milk
1 qt. boiling water
Table salt
2 eggs, beaten
2 tbsp. water
1 cup Italian-style breadcrumbs
Oil for frying

Add one junket or rennet tablet to 2 quarts sweet milk. Let the milk set until it clabbers, or curdles. Break up clabber. Pour 1 quart boiling water over clabber. Pour everything into a gauze or cheesecloth bag while holding bag over a large pot. Squeeze all water from clabber. Remove cheese from bag and pat table salt over it. Lightly beat eggs with water. Slice cheese into 8 equal portions, dip in beaten eggs and breadcrumbs, and fry in hot oil until lightly browned and crisp. Drain and serve. The cheese can also be used on pizza and pasta. To store cheese, place in a jar, cover, and refrigerate in the summer. You can keep it out in the winter. Makes 8 servings.

Variation:
For soft ricotta add 2 quarts sweet milk to the water drained from clabber. Bring to a boil. Add 1 tablespoon vinegar and stir well. Ricotta will rise to the top. Turn fire off. Dip out ricotta with slotted spoon or strainer. Do not salt this cheese. It will keep in the refrigerator for about 2 weeks. Makes 1 cup ricotta.

Aunt Lena's Homemade Ricotta

Ricotta is a very fine cottage-like cheese used in many Italian dishes. Aunt Lena Fertitta Culotta of Leesville, Louisiana, shared her recipe. With 5 children in the house, Aunt Lena's ricotta did not have to be salted; it was used very quickly in a variety of ways to feed family and share with friends.

2 gal. homogenized milk
1 qt. buttermilk

Heat milk in a heavy pot until it begins to bubble. Turn heat to low and stir milk so it won't scorch. While stirring, slowly add the buttermilk. The milk will curdle, and ricotta will rise to the top. Let it stand a minute then scoop the cheese out with a slotted spoon or drain in a cheesecloth bag. Makes about 4 cups ricotta.

Mozzarella Appetizer

Paul Arrigo likes to fix this appetizer for his army of Italian relatives from Chalmette. Paul and his brother, Frank, are active members of the Italian American Marching Club based in Baton Rouge.

1 lb. fresh whole milk mozzarella, cubed
2 tbsp. extra virgin olive oil
2 tsp. white wine balsamic vinegar
¼ tsp. salt
3 tsp. chopped fresh basil

Place all ingredients in a small casserole dish. Stir well. Cover and refrigerate for several hours before serving. Serve with your favorite crackers. Makes 30 pieces.

Prosciutto with Melon

My favorite antipasto is at the famous Italian restaurant, Leoni's, in New York. There, prosciutto, or Italian ham, is served with fresh figs, which are abundant in Louisiana. This dish might sound like a delicacy to some, but here in Louisiana there is hardly a family who doesn't have a fig tree in the backyard or knows someone who does.

1 cantaloupe or honeydew melon
½ lb. prosciutto, thinly sliced
Black pepper, freshly ground
12 large ripe figs

Chill melon. Cut in half and remove seeds then cut along skin but do not detach. Cut melon into ¾-inch slices. Place prosciutto over slices and top with freshly ground black pepper. Wash and chill figs. Peel and split. Top with prosciutto and freshly ground black pepper. Chill until ready to serve. Makes 8 servings.

Best Cocktail Meatballs

Rosemary Reynolds, a wonderful cook and friend, shared this recipe with me many years ago. It takes a bit of extra time but is well worth the effort. More than one of my Italian friends has shared the secret that "a little pork in a dish" makes a great difference in flavor.

3 lb. ground beef
1 lb. ground pork
3 cups plain breadcrumbs
3 eggs
1½ cups water
1 tbsp. lemon juice
2 tsp. Worcestershire sauce
2 tsp. soy sauce
2 tsp. barbecue sauce
1 tsp. garlic salt
1 tsp. celery salt
1 tsp. salt
1 tsp. black pepper
1 tbsp. Italian seasoning
¼ tsp. thyme
1 tbsp. hickory smoke flavor

Sauce
½ cup catsup
½ cup burgundy
3 cups bottled hickory barbecue sauce
1½ cups water

Place meats in a large bowl. Sprinkle breadcrumbs over meat and mix well with hand. Add eggs and water. Mix well. Add remaining ingredients and mix well. Form into small meatballs. Place on a shallow tray and bake at 350 degrees until browned. Combine sauce ingredients. Pour over meatballs and serve. Makes 100 1-ounce meatballs.

Vegetables and Sides

Stuffed Bell Peppers

The "saints" are the only people who taste everything on the altar. The menu for visitors usually consists of pasta with gravy, vegetable omelets, fried vegetables, bread, maybe salad, and cookies to take home. Wine, soft drinks, and sometimes beer are served. Other foods often included are stuffed crabs, stuffed artichokes, boiled crawfish, crabs, shrimp, and red beans and rice for those who might not care for the usual flavor of St. Joseph Gravy. You'll want to use small vegetables for your St. Joseph table if a great variety of food is to be served.

1 small onion, minced
1 large clove garlic, minced
1½ lb. shrimp, peeled, deveined, and chopped
1 tbsp. olive oil
1 cup breadcrumbs
⅓ cup Parmesan cheese, grated
1 egg
1½ tsp. oregano
1 tsp. salt
¼ tsp. black pepper or ⅛ tsp. red pepper
3 bell peppers, split with seeds and membrane removed

Breadcrumb Topping
2 tbsp. melted butter
½ cup plain breadcrumbs

Sauté onions, garlic, and shrimp in oil. Add breadcrumbs, cheese, egg, and seasoning. Mix well. Cut peppers in half lengthwise. Remove stems and seeds. Parboil until skins turn a little dull in color; they should still be firm. Stuff with shrimp mixture. Mix melted butter and breadcrumbs to create the breadcrumb topping. Spread about 1 tablespoon topping on each stuffed pepper half. Bake at 350 degrees for 30 to 35 minutes. Makes 6 stuffed halves.

Stewed Fresh Bell Peppers

Lucky Lynda Perry of Baton Rouge received a gift for her sister's birthday. Her brother, Earl Marter of Shreveport, gave his wife and sister a trip to Florence, Italy, for a 2-week cooking school. The teacher was Signora Enrica Jarratt, a Cordon Bleu chef and owner of George's, at that time one of the most famous restaurants in Rome. Here in Baton Rouge, Mrs. Perry and a friend, Sue Brown, taught classes in Chinese, French, Cajun, soul, and crepe cooking back in the seventies. Mrs. Perry contributed this recipe, which is called *pepperonata* in Italian.

3½ lb. bell peppers, skinned, peeled, and seeded
3 tbsp. oil
½ medium onion, sliced
1 clove of garlic, crushed
3 large tomatoes, skins removed
¼ tsp. salt
¼ tsp. black pepper

Cook the peppers in a frying pan with a little very hot oil until the skin blisters so that peppers can be peeled. Cut them in pieces and take out the seeds. Warm 3 tablespoons of oil in a pan, add the onion and garlic, and sauté gently for 5 minutes. Add the peppers and fry for 5 minutes. Then add tomatoes, salt, and pepper. Reduce heat. Cover pan and simmer 30 minutes. Makes 6 servings.

Hint
To remove tomato skins, place tomatoes on tines of a fork, dip in boiling water then ice cold water. The change in water temperature will cause skins to split and slip off easily.

Cabbage Casserole

This recipe from the Cornelius family of Baton Rouge combines some ingredients you might not have thought of putting together.

1 large onion, chopped
1 large clove garlic, minced
1 tbsp. olive oil
1 lb. shrimp, peeled, deveined, and chopped
1 medium head of cabbage
1 8-oz. can tomato sauce
¾ cup Parmesan cheese

Sauté onion and garlic in olive oil. Add chopped shrimp to the onion and garlic mixture. Cook until shrimp turn pink. Add tomato sauce to shrimp. Cut cabbage into pieces and lightly steam in a little water. Layer cabbage, shrimp and tomato sauce mixture, and cheese in casserole dish, ending with cheese as the top layer. Bake at 350 degrees for about 25 minutes. Makes 8 servings.

Holiday Fritters

Vegetable fritters, called *sfingi*, and vegetable omelets are often served with pasta and gravy to those who attend the St. Joseph altars. Vegetables of all kinds can be prepared this way.

1 cup broccoli
1 cup cauliflower flowerets
1 cup carduna, or artichoke stems, parboiled and cubed
1 small eggplant, cut into 1-inch cubes
1 medium yellow squash, cut into 1-inch cubes
1 mirliton, parboiled and cubed
1 13½- or 16-oz can artichoke hearts
1 cup all-purpose flour
½ tsp. pepper
1 cup milk
1 tbsp. melted fat, butter, or bacon fat
1 egg white

Prepare broccoli and cauliflower by washing, breaking into flowerets, and parboiling. Peel carduna (artichoke stems). Cut into small pieces and parboil. Peel, dice, and parboil eggplant, squash, and mirlitons. Cook eggplant until it becomes soft. Dip canned artichoke hearts into batter. Combine all ingredients, except vegetables, and beat well. Dip vegetables into batter. Fry in hot oil, about 375 degrees on a deep fryer, and cook about three minutes until light brown. Makes 20 servings.

Cauliflower Frittata

Mrs. A. J. Teracina of Opelousas, Louisiana, sent this recipe for fried cauliflower. She says that vegetables are a must for an altar and that cabbage and broccoli can also be prepared in this manner.

2 heads cauliflower
1 gal. water
1 tsp. salt
2 tbsp. olive oil
10 eggs
Salt, pepper, and hot sauce to taste (optional)

Clean cauliflower and cut each head into about 4 pieces. Boil water in a large pot. Add cauliflower and salt. Cook until tender but not too soft. Drain on absorbent paper. Let olive oil heat in 12-inch frying pan then put in cauliflower and fry for 5 to 10 minutes. Remove cauliflower from oil and drain. Place in a clean pan or oven-safe dish. Beat eggs then pour over cauliflower. Cook in a pan over low heat or bake in oven at 350 degrees until eggs are done. Season with salt, pepper, and hot sauce if desired. Place a large serving platter over cooked cauliflower and turn over so that cauliflower will be evenly spread on the dish. Serve hot. Makes 10 servings.

Boiled Cauliflower Soup

The frugality of the early days lives on in the children of this era. While I was making frittatas, one of my "little old lady" friends scavenged small pieces of cauliflower and leaves that I was going to discard and made a lovely cauliflower soup.

4 cups cauliflower pieces and leaves
1 cup white beans, cooked and drained
2 qt. chicken broth
½ cup Parmesan or Romano cheese
¼ tsp. pepper
¼ tsp. salt

Rinse cauliflower. Place in a 3-quart pot with beans and bring to a boil. Boil until cauliflower is just tender. Stir in cheese. Season with pepper and salt. Makes 8 servings.

Cannizzaro Fried Cauliflower

My good friend Cheryl Cannizzaro Faust sent this recipe, a family favorite. Her children like cauliflower prepared this way and sprinkled with Parmesan cheese. They like the cheese on everything, even eggs!

1 cup flour
1 tsp. Italian seasoning
½ tsp. salt
¼ tsp. black pepper
1 large head cauliflower, cut into florets and parboiled
Vegetable oil for frying
⅓ cup Parmesan cheese

Place flour and seasonings in a 1-quart plastic bag. Shake. Place a few pieces of cauliflower in the bag at a time and thoroughly flour each piece. Remove from bag and shake off excess flour. Fry in hot oil (375 degrees) until golden brown. Drain. Sprinkle with cheese and serve. Makes 10 servings.

Risotto Milanese or Risotto Zafferano

Josie Bonura of St. Rose says her family loves this dish, which her mother used to make for the St. Joseph altar. True to form, nothing is too good for St. Joseph. One ounce of saffron requires more than 4,000 flowers, so saffron is the most expensive spice in the world.

¼ cup onion, finely chopped
1 tbsp. olive oil or butter
2¼ cups water
1 cup rice, uncooked and washed
1 chicken bouillon cube
⅛ tsp. saffron
½ cup Parmesan cheese, freshly grated
1 small head cauliflower, parboiled and broken into small pieces

Brown onions in oil or butter. Add 2 cups water, rice, and bouillon cube. Dissolve saffron in ¼ cup water. Strain and add saffron liquid to rice. Bring rice and water to a boil over low heat. Cover and cook until rice is tender. Serve drizzled with additional olive oil and cheese. Arrange cauliflower along edges of dish. Makes 8 servings.

Creamed Spinach

This recipe has been a family favorite for years. It is great when you can pick fresh spinach from the garden, but frozen spinach works well, too.

2 10-oz. packages frozen spinach
4 tbsp. butter
3 tbsp. flour
2 cups milk or half and half
8 slices bacon, chopped and fried crisp; reserve fat
4 tbsp. chopped onion
1/2 tsp. salt
1/4 tsp. black pepper
1/8 tsp. nutmeg

Thaw spinach and squeeze out liquid. Melt butter in skillet. Mix in flour and cook for 4 minutes, stirring constantly. Whisk in milk or half and half. Whisk until smooth. Bring to a boil, cook 3 minutes, and set aside. Brown onion in 2 tablespoons bacon fat. Drain. Place spinach, bacon, and onion in cream sauce. Add seasonings. Makes 8 servings.

Eggplant "Quails"

When Shirley Dauzat of Baton Rouge gave me a frozen container of these, I, very frankly, was not impressed. It wasn't until I thawed the contents, thinking I would have soup, that I realized that I had frozen eggplants in a red sauce. I prepared them as Shirley had directed and couldn't stop raving about them.

Salt
4 small eggplants
2 cloves garlic, cut into 16 slices
1/2 cup Romano cheese, sliced
1/2 lb. ham or 8 anchovies
Olive oil for sautéing

Wash, peel, and salt small eggplants. Leave whole. Score 4 times almost to center. Place garlic, cheese, and ham or anchovies inside cuts. Tie with thin thread. Brown eggplants slowly in good olive oil. Prepare your favorite Italian gravy. When the gravy is half cooked, add eggplants and continue cooking until eggplant is tender. Be sure to season gravy with Parmesan or Romano cheese. Makes 4 servings.

Eggplant Casserole

1 large eggplant
1 cup milk
1 egg
1 cup flour
Oil for frying
1 medium onion, chopped
1 bell pepper, chopped
1 lb. ground beef
2 6-oz. cans tomato sauce
½ can water
½ tsp. oregano
½ tsp. salt
¼ tsp. pepper
1 cup cheddar cheese, grated

Cut eggplant in large strips. Mix milk and egg to make an egg wash. Dip eggplant in egg wash then in flour. Fry eggplant in hot oil until brown. Sauté onion and bell pepper. Add ground meat and brown well. Add tomato sauce, water, oregano, salt, and pepper. In a casserole dish, layer meat with eggplant and sauce. Top with 1 cup of grated cheddar cheese. Bake at 350 degrees for 30 minutes. Makes 8 servings.

Fava Beans

The dried fava bean is the "lucky" bean given to those attending the St. Joseph altars. Keep one with you for prosperity. Dolores Sardegna Faucheux, whose family came from the island of Sardegna, has them all over her house.

1 medium onion, finely chopped
1 tbsp. olive oil
1 rib celery, finely chopped
1 8-oz. can tomato sauce.
1 20-oz can fava beans.

Sauté onion in oil. Add remaining ingredients, including liquid from beans. Simmer over low heat for approximately 25 minutes, stirring occasionally. Eat alone or serve with spaghetti. Makes 6 servings.

Old-Fashioned Fennel Greens

1 bunch fresh fennel, cut into 1-inch pieces
1 gal. water
2 tsp. salt
1 head cauliflower, broken into flowerets and parboiled
2 qt. your favorite tomato sauce

Break away the tough outside pieces of fennel and wash the fennel several times. Boil with salt for about 30 minutes or until tender. Drain the fennel in a colander and put the fennel greens in a roasting pan along with parboiled cauliflower. Spread your favorite tomato sauce over the vegetables. Bake at 350 degrees for about 45 minutes. Makes 20 servings.

Mushroom Casserole

Mushroom farms can now be found in south Louisiana along with artisan cheese dairies, dairies that make cheese with natural cultures and no preservatives, and hearth-bread bakeries. This is an especially good casserole for mushroom lovers.

4 slices white or brown bread
1/2 cup milk or half and half
2 garlic cloves, smashed
6 tbsp. extra virgin olive oil
1 lb. mushrooms
3 tomatoes, peeled and diced
4 eggs
1/2 cup Parmesan cheese
1/4 tsp. Italian seasoning
1/4 tsp. salt
1/4 tsp. black pepper

Moisten bread with milk or half and half. Sauté garlic in oil. Stir in mushrooms and tomatoes. Cook for approximately 10 minutes. While mushrooms and tomatoes are cooking, beat eggs until light. Blend cheese and moist bread into eggs. Add about 3/4 of the mushroom mix to the bread mix. Place in a 2-quart buttered casserole dish and top with remaining mushroom mix. Bake at 350 degrees for about 15 minutes. Makes 4 servings.

Pasta con Broccoli

Many Italian families held tightly to the old traditions of Italy. The Marino family was no different. Children worked in the fields to help the family. Fathers chose husbands for their daughters despite the customs of America. The story is that in the Marino family, one of the daughters was introduced to her chosen husband while digging potatoes in the fields. Later she married the young man and had 13 children. Here is Shirley (Marino) Dauzat's Broccoli and Pasta recipe.

2 qt. water
2½ tsp. salt
1 lb. frozen broccoli cuts or fresh broccoli, cut into small pieces
1 lb. pasta (I use shell macaroni, but any small pasta will do.)
⅓ cup olive oil
½ cup grated Parmesan cheese

Bring water to a boil and season with salt. Add broccoli and cook until tender. Drain broccoli but reserve the water for cooking pasta. Add pasta to broccoli water and cook until almost tender. Drain and reserve about 2 cups liquid. Combine cooked broccoli and pasta. Pour reserved liquid over the pasta and drizzle with olive oil. Sprinkle with Parmesan cheese. Makes 9 servings.

Yellow Squash with Bacon

2 slices of bacon, diced
3 tbsp. chopped onion
Oil for sautéing
4 small yellow squash
¼ tsp. salt
⅛ tsp. black pepper

Fry bacon then remove from pan. Add onions and sauté for about 3 minutes. Add yellow squash and bacon pieces. Stir. Cover, reduce heat, and cook until squash is tender, stirring occasionally. Season with salt and black pepper. Makes 4 servings.

Lentil Soup

My mother-in-law called these "lenteges." Perhaps lenteges is the corruption of the dish's Italian name, which she remembered from her childhood. Lentils are a common dish in the Far East and are available in several colors, though they all cook out to tan. In Louisiana these bland little beans were doctored up in the Southern tradition with onions, smoked sausage, celery, and hot sauce.

2 tbsp. butter
1 tbsp. olive oil
½ cup onion, chopped
1 carrot, peeled and chopped
1 rib celery, chopped
1 smoked pork chop, deboned and diced
½ lb. lentils
1 lb. crushed tomatoes
1½ qt. water
2 tsp. salt
¼ tsp. black pepper
2 tbsp. chopped parsley

Heat butter and oil in a 2-quart pot. Add onion, carrot, and celery. Cook about 10 minutes. Add smoked pork chop, lentils, tomato, water, and salt. Bring to a boil, reduce heat, and cover. Simmer 1½ hours or until lentils are as tender as desired. Add pepper and parsley. Makes 4 servings.

Zucchini-Tomato Sauté

1 small onion, sliced
1 clove garlic, minced
1 tbsp. olive oil
3 cups zucchini, cubed
¼ tsp. salt
¼ tsp. pepper
½ tsp. dried oregano
1 cup cherry tomatoes

Sauté onion and garlic in olive oil for 5 minutes. Add zucchini and cook for another 5 minutes. Add salt, pepper, oregano, and tomatoes and stir well. Cook 3 additional minutes. Serve hot. Makes 6 servings.

Zucchini Salad

2 lb. zucchini, cubed
1/2 cup olive oil
1 tbsp. wine vinegar
1 clove garlic, mashed
1/4 tsp. salt
1/4 tsp. black pepper

Place all ingredients in a large bowl. Toss. Makes 6 servings.

Stuffed Turnips

Edwina B. Robinson has had many St. Joseph altars. She likes to give each visitor something to take home, so lucky beans, bread, a prayer card, and a metal are wrapped and given to her visitors. She decorates her table with all types of fruit, including watermelon, pumpkins, and cantaloupes. Red, she said, is the main color used for decorating the altar.

8 turnips
Salted water for boiling
1/2 cup butter
1 large onion, chopped
1 cup fresh tomatoes, peeled and chopped
1 tsp. salt
1 tsp. caraway seeds
1 tsp. sugar

Peel turnips. Remove centers to make hollow "shells." After removing, chop the turnip centers. Cook turnip shells in boiling, salted water for about 30 minutes. Drain and cool. Melt butter in large skillet. Add onions and chopped turnip. Sauté until tender then remove from heat. Add tomatoes, salt, caraway seeds, and sugar. Season shells lightly with salt. Fill with stuffing. Place in baking dish and bake at 350 degrees for 15 to 20 minutes. Makes 8 servings.

Green Beans and Potatoes

Potatoes show up in unusual places in ethnic cuisine. This is true in the Italian kitchens in Louisiana. The traditional recipe combines potatoes with the extra-long green bean known as the Italian green bean. However, this recipe is good with any type green bean and, as a shortcut, you can use canned green beans.

2 slices bacon
½ cup finely chopped onion
1 small clove garlic
2 14.5-oz. cans green beans
2 small potatoes, peeled and cubed
2 tbsp. cornstarch
⅓ cup water
¼ tsp. salt
⅛ tsp. black pepper

Fry bacon in a skillet until crisp. Add onion and garlic. Continue cooking for 4 minutes. Add green beans with liquid and potatoes. Stir well to deglaze pan. Cook 10 minutes or until potatoes are tender. Mix cornstarch with water and stir into green beans. Continue to cook on low heat until sauce has thickened. Serve as a side dish or use ½ pound sliced smoked pork sausage in place of bacon and serve as a main dish. Season with salt and pepper. Makes 4 servings.

Gnocchi

We just call them potato dumplings, but to my Italian friends they are "noke-ee." These are a great accompaniment to roasted rabbit.

3 lb. Idaho potatoes
Water to cover
1 tsp. salt
¼ cup butter or olive oil
2 egg yolks
3¾ cups all-purpose flour
⅛ tsp. nutmeg

Wash potatoes. Place in a large pot and cover with water. Add salt. Boil water and cook until potatoes are soft. Drain potatoes and place in mixer bowl. Beat smooth. Add melted butter or olive oil and quickly beat in egg yolks. Place in large skillet and cook until dough gets very stiff. Remove from heat and add flour a little at a time as, using a plastic scraper, you knead the hot dough to mix in flour. Divide the dough into 6 pieces and roll each piece into a snakelike form. Cut into 1/2-inch pieces. Roll in palms of hands to shape into an elongated ball. Place on a baking sheet or waxed paper to dry. Cook as you would pasta or freeze for later use. Do not thaw to cook. Makes 10 servings.

Spinach Gnocchi

Gnocchi can be served as a side dish or a main dish. This is a particularly good recipe from the Passarella family.

1 bunch spinach (about 8 oz.)
3 tbsp. water
8 oz. ricotta
3 oz. grated Parmesan cheese
1/4 tsp. salt
1 egg
1/4 tsp. black pepper
1/4 tsp. nutmeg
Flour
Water for boiling
3 tbsp. butter

Wash and dry spinach. Remove coarse ribs. Cook spinach with 3 tablespoons water for 5 minutes. Drain well and chop into fine pieces. Combine spinach with ricotta, 1 1/2 ounces Parmesan cheese, salt, egg, pepper, and nutmeg. Mix well. Form mixture into balls or egg shapes using a tablespoon and palm of your hand. Roll gnocchi in flour. Bring a large pot of water to a boil and drop in gnocchi 3 or 4 at a time. Simmer until the gnocchi rise to the top of the water. Remove with a slotted spoon and place in oven-safe dish. Melt butter and pour over gnocchi. Sprinkle with remaining Parmesan cheese. Place under broiler until cheese browns lightly. Makes 8 servings.

Oven-Roasted Italian Potatoes

No matter how many servings of this dish I cook, there never seems to be enough. I first tasted these potatoes at a dinner cooked at Judge Mary Ann Lemmon's home. Mary Ann is an old friend with whom I have been cooking since our 4-H Club days. She is a terrific cook, a mother of 6, and a federal judge appointed by Pres. Bill Clinton.

3 lb. white potatoes, washed
1/3 cup extra-virgin olive oil
1/2 tsp. salt
1/2 tsp. black pepper
1 1/2 tsp. Italian seasoning

Do not peel potatoes. Cut potatoes into 1-inch cubes. Place in a heavy roaster and sprinkle with oil and seasonings. Mix to coat potatoes. Bake 35 to 40 minutes until potatoes are tender and nicely browned. Makes 10 servings.

Potato-Cheese Balls

Bertha Culmone said several hundred people sometimes showed up to pay respect to St. Joseph at her altar. Can you imagine the pounds of potatoes she used to feed them these delicious potato balls? She said that one year she made Potato-Cheese Balls with 70 pounds of potatoes.

2 cups potatoes, boiled and washed
3/4 cup Romano or Parmesan cheese, grated
1 egg
1 clove garlic, mashed
4 tbsp. minced onion
1/2 tsp. salt
1/4 black pepper
1 cup Italian (or plain) breadcrumbs
Oil for frying

Peel, boil, and mash potatoes. Add cheese, egg, garlic, onion, salt, and pepper. Shape into balls and fry until lightly browned. They are good reheated, too. Makes 8 balls.

Polenta

The Cajuns in south Louisiana call this *couscous.* Calling the recipe *polenta* gives a continental flair to this country dish.

3½ cups water
¾ cup finely ground yellow corn meal
½ tsp. salt
⅛ tsp. black pepper

Bring water to a boil. Add corn meal, salt, and pepper. Return to a boil. Cover and cook on low heat until polenta is thick but still loose enough to pour. Serve or pour into a small buttered casserole dish. Serve with meat sauce or slice and fry in olive oil until nicely browned. Makes 6 servings.

Polenta with Eggs

Italy has polenta with eggs; Louisiana has grits and eggs.

8 slices polenta
3 tbsp. oil
8 eggs.
Butter for frying
¼ tsp. salt
¼ tsp. pepper

Cut cooled polenta in ½-inch-thick slices. Fry polenta in hot oil on both sides. Fry eggs on low heat in butter. Season with salt and pepper. Slide one egg on each slice of polenta. Serve hot. Makes 4 servings.

Rice and Milk

This is not sweet rice pudding but rice cooked with milk and butter, making it a savory side dish or cereal.

4 cups milk
2 cups long-grain rice
¼ cup butter
2 tsp. salt

Bring milk to a boil. Add rice, butter, and salt. Return to a boil, cover, and cook on low for approximately 20 minutes. Serve with meat as a side dish or add additional milk to serve as a hot breakfast cereal. Makes 8 servings.

Rice Balls

(*Arancini*)

My mother-in-law, Angelina Culotta Wilson, did not particularly like to cook. To avoid cooking for events, she would buy a Mrs. Smith's pie and have her neighbor, Mrs. Smith, bake it for her. When the thermostat went out on her oven, she didn't bother to have it replaced. She was in her late '60s when this happened; she was 92 when she died, and she never did get the oven fixed! To her credit, Angelina always had pasta and sauce or lentil soup waiting for us on arrival at her house, and she did take time to teach me some of the family specialties like arancini. She made these rice balls for holiday celebrations.

2 cups short grain rice, uncooked
4½ cups water
2 tsp. salt
4 egg yolks, slightly beaten
4 egg whites, whipped frothy
2 cups plain breadcrumbs

Place rice, water, and salt in a 4-quart pot. Bring water to a boil. Cover, reduce heat, and cook for 20 minutes or until rice is tender. Rice will be sticky. Cool. Add egg yolks and stir well. Divide into 8 equal portions and form small balls. Set aside.

Filling
1 lb. lean ground beef
1 large onion, finely chopped
2 ribs celery, finely chopped
1 6-oz. can tomato paste
2 cups hot water
1½ tsp. oregano
1 tsp. salt
¼ tsp. black pepper
2 tbsp. chili powder
⅛ tsp. cinnamon
½ tsp. powdered garlic

Brown beef. Add onion and celery and cook over low heat for 10 minutes. Add remaining ingredients. Simmer 25 minutes. Holding the rice ball in the palm of your hand, make a well in the center.

Place a tablespoon of filling in the hole. Mold rice around filling and shape into a ball. Roll in egg whites then in breadcrumbs. Repeat for each portion of rice. Chill for 1 hour before frying. Heat oil to 375 degrees. Fry balls 3 at a time in deep fryer, turning each to brown evenly. Serve alone or with remaining filling. Makes 8 rice balls.

Rice Croquettes of the Telephone

These little rice balls, a recipe from Kara Gutierrez's in-laws in Florence, are called *suppli al telefono* in Italian. The name comes from the fact that the cheese pulls apart like telephone wires after the balls are broken apart.

4 tbsp. butter
1 small onion, chopped
1/4 cup dry white wine
1 cup hot water
Pinch of saffron
1 chicken bouillon cube
1 tsp. salt
1/4 tsp. black pepper
1 1/2 cups long-grain rice
1 tbsp. grated Parmesan cheese
2 eggs
4 oz. Mozzarella cheese
1/4 cup plain breadcrumbs
Oil for frying

Heat 2 tablespoons butter in a small skillet. Add onion and cook for about 10 minutes. Add wine, 1/2 cup hot water, saffron, bouillon, salt, and pepper. Bring to a boil, add rice, and stir well. When water has almost evaporated, add remaining water. Reduce heat and cook uncovered until water has been absorbed, about 15 minutes. Stir in extra butter and Parmesan cheese. Beat eggs. Add to rice mixture and stir gently with a fork. Cut the mozzarella into 1/2-inch cubes. Place a tablespoon of rice in 1 hand, add a cube of cheese, and then cover the cheese with another tablespoon of rice. Pat the mixture into a ball. Roll the ball in breadcrumbs. Refrigerate for at least 2 hours. Fry in hot oil for about 5 minutes or until nicely browned. Makes 6 servings.

Rice with Peas

Rice with Peas, or *Risi e Bisi,* finds company with red beans and rice in south Louisiana. This is not risotto but more akin to a soupy hopping John.

2 slices bacon
¼ cup butter
1 small onion, minced
3 lb. fresh peas
1 oz. parsley
1 qt. beef broth
8 oz. long-grain rice

Fry bacon in a skillet until crisp then discard grease. Crumble bacon. Place butter and onion in skillet and cook until lightly browned or about 10 minutes. Add crumbled bacon and remaining ingredients. Bring to a boil. Reduce heat and cook for approximately 20 minutes until rice is tender. This should be a soupy dish. Add additional broth to achieve desired consistency. Makes 18 servings.

Catalonian Rice Salad

1 cup rice, cooked
1 red bell pepper
1 green bell pepper
2 oz. seedless raisins
1 cup green pitted olives
1 tbsp. chopped parsley
2 oz. currants
5 oz. toasted almonds
8 tbsp. olive oil
3 tbsp. white wine vinegar
¼ tsp. salt
⅛ tsp. black pepper

Rinse rice in cold water and drain well. Remove seeds from peppers and dice. Put rice in salad bowl with bell pepper, raisins, olives, parsley, currants, and almonds. Mix well. Combine olive oil, vinegar, salt, and pepper and pour over salad 10 minutes before serving. Makes 4 servings.

Artichoke Rice

Castroville, California, might be the artichoke production capital of the world, but Louisiana must surely be the "artichoke lovers capital." Stuffed, marinated, "souped," or "casseroled," they have even found their way into the crawfish-boiling pots in south Louisiana.

3 tbsp. olive oil
1 small onion, chopped
2 cloves garlic, minced
1 10-oz. package frozen artichoke hearts
½ tsp salt
¼ tsp. black pepper
3 fresh Roma tomatoes, chopped
1 tsp. marjoram
½ tsp. oregano
1 cup long-grain rice, uncooked
2 cups water or unseasoned chicken broth
⅓ cup Italian cheese blend
¼ cup Kalamata olives, chopped

Heat olive oil. Add onion and cook for about 3 minutes. Add garlic, artichoke hearts, salt, and pepper and sauté for about 5 minutes. Stir in tomatoes, marjoram, and oregano. Add rice, water, cheese, and olives. Bring to a boil. Cover and cook over low heat for about 25 minutes or until rice is cooked through. Makes 6 to 8 servings.

Angelo's Pear and Walnut Salad

1 Asian pear or Gala apple, diced
¼ cup walnut pieces
¼ cup whole white beans, cooked and rinsed
4 cups commercial mixed greens
¼ cup olive oil
2 tbsp. balsamic vinegar
2 tbsp. water
½ tsp. sugar
¼ cup Gorgonzola, crumbled

Peel and cube pear or apple. Place fruit, walnuts, beans, and greens in a large bowl. Toss. Mix oil, vinegar, water, and sugar together. Pour over greens. Sprinkle cheese over greens. Makes 2 servings.

Frank's Italian Salad

Frank Porretto of Houma, Louisiana, besides being a successful businessman, also is known for his successful ventures in the kitchen. A little practice with these ingredients and you should be able to come up with a salad as delectable as his.

8 oz. prepared Italian dressing, oil and vinegar style
10 marinated artichoke hearts, quartered
4 oz. Romano cheese, freshly grated
6 oz. summer salami, julienne or cut into 1-inch squares
1 head lettuce, torn into bite-size pieces
2 ribs celery, diced
1 bell pepper, cut in strips
10 pepperoncini peppers
½ cup black olives, pitted
1 small cauliflower, parboiled and broken into small pieces
2 tomatoes, cut into wedges
1 avocado, diced

Place Italian dressing, artichoke hearts, cheese, and salami in large salad bowl to marinate for 2 hours. Immediately before serving, add lettuce, celery, and bell pepper strips. Mix lightly to coat ingredients with dressing. Add pepperoncini peppers, black olives, and cauliflower, which should be crisp and drained. Add tomatoes and avocado. Toss lightly to coat all ingredients well. Serve immediately. Makes 12 servings.

Italian Salad Dressing

½ cup olive
1½ tsp. salt
1 clove garlic, minced
½ tsp. powdered mustard
4 tbsp. wine vinegar
½ tsp. dried oregano
¼ tsp. black pepper

Combine all ingredients in a jar. Cover and shake well. Let stand for several hours before serving. Makes ¾ cups dressing.

Pasta and Savory Sauces

Lasagna

This perennial favorite is a good casserole to serve to a large group of people.

1/4 cup olive oil
2 cloves garlic, mashed
1/3 cup tomato paste
1/2 cup hot water
1 28-oz. can Italian plum tomatoes
1 rib celery
1/2 tsp. salt
1/8 tsp. pepper
1 lb. Italian sausage
1 1/2 lb. lasagna noodles
1 1/2 cups grated Parmesan cheese
1 1/2 cups mozzarella cheese, cubed
1 1/2 lb. ricotta

Heat oil in a skillet. Add garlic and sauté for 3 minutes. Blend tomato paste with hot water and add to garlic in skillet. Add tomatoes, celery, salt, and pepper. Mix well and bring to a boil. Reduce heat and simmer covered for about 1 hour. Broil sausage about 10 minutes or until well browned. Cut sausage in 1-inch pieces. Cook noodles and drain. Pour 1 1/2 cups sauce in the bottom of a 9-inch by 13-inch casserole dish. Arrange noodles over sauce. Layer noodles with cheese, meat, and sauce. Repeat layers, ending with cheese as the top layer. Bake at 350 degrees for about 20 minutes or until set. Makes 6 servings.

Baked Manicotti

Mary Anzalone of Independence sent her favorite manicotti recipe. This dish can be prepared and refrigerated then baked immediately before serving.

Sauce
1 large onion, finely chopped
1/4 cup olive oil
1 clove garlic, crushed
1 35-oz. can Italian tomatoes
1 6-oz. can tomato paste
1 1/2 cups water
2 sprigs parsley
1 tsp. salt
1 tsp. dried oregano leaves
1/2 tsp. dried basil leaves
1/4 tsp. red pepper
1/4 tsp. black pepper
2 tsp. sugar
14 manicotti shells
Salted water for boiling

In a 6-quart pot, sauté onion in oil until golden brown; add garlic, and cook over low heat for 3 minutes. Add remaining ingredients, except manicotti shells. Mix well, making sure to mash tomatoes. Bring to a boil. Simmer uncovered 1 hour, stirring occasionally. Preheat oven to 350 degrees. Boil shells in salted water until tender. Drain.

Filling
2 lb. ricotta cheese
8 oz. mozzarella cheese, diced
1/3 cup grated Parmesan cheese
2 eggs
1 tbsp. chopped parsley
Salt
1 tsp. pepper

Mix cheeses, eggs, parsley, salt, and pepper. Place about 1/4 cup filling in each shell. Spoon some of the tomato sauce into the bottom of a 9-inch by 13-inch casserole dish. Place stuffed shells on sauce. Cover with remaining sauce. Bake uncovered about 30 minutes in a 350-degree oven for about 30 minutes. Makes 4 servings.

Fettuccine Alfredo

I couldn't write an Italian book without sharing this all-time favorite. The biggest mistake that most people make is failing to salt the water in which pasta is cooked. Salting after cooking is not the same!

Salted water for boiling
1 lb. fettuccine
4 tbsp. butter
2 tbsp. flour
3/4 cup grated Parmesan or Romano cheese
1 1/2 cups half and half
1/8 tsp. nutmeg
1/8 tsp. salt
1/4 tsp. black pepper

Cook fettuccine in a pot of salted water until al dente. Be sure to let the water come to a boil before adding pasta. When pasta is cooked, drain water and set aside. Melt butter in a heavy skillet. Add flour and cook for about 3 minutes. Add half and half. Beat with a wire whisk until flour is absorbed into the liquid and liquid is smooth. Add cheese, nutmeg, salt, and pepper and stir. Pour over noodles. Makes 6 to 8 servings.

Shrimp Fettuccine

The name of this dish has become synonymous with any creamy shrimp and pasta dish regardless of the type of pasta used.

1/2 cup flour
4 tbsp. butter or margarine, melted
2 cups milk
1 tbsp. dehydrated onions
1 tsp. dehydrated parsley
1 cup mild cheddar cheese, grated
1/4 cup Parmesan cheese, grated
1 lb. precooked shrimp
1/2 lb. fettuccine noodles, cooked

Add flour to melted butter and cook for 3 minutes. Whisk in milk, onion, and parsley. Bring to a boil, reduce heat, and cook 5 minutes, stirring constantly. Add cheeses and stir until cheese is melted. Add shrimp and noodles. Makes 6 servings.

Spaghetti with Tuna

When I first heard about this dish, I did not image that it would be delectable—but it is!

1/4 cup olive oil
1/2 cup butter
6 or 7 oz. canned tuna
1/4 cup chopped fresh parsley
3 tbsp. water,
1 lb. spaghetti, cooked

Combine oil, butter, and parsley in a small skillet. Heat until butter melts. Add tuna and cook about 5 minutes. Add water and simmer over low heat for 10 minutes. Pour over hot, cooked spaghetti. Makes 8 servings.

Pasta alla Puttanesca

This 20-minute sauce is so good it will fool anyone into believing that you slaved over it all day. My friend Kara Gutierrez says that when she visited her husband's relatives in Italy, this dish was served. When complimented, her husband's aunt replied, "Ah, pasta alla puttanesca," and everyone laughed. It was only after she got home that her husband explained that *puttanesca* means "slut" in Italian. The joke was that it didn't take much time to make the sauce. You could go out all day, but your husband would think you were home slaving over the stove to make this wonderful sauce for him.

4 tomatoes
2 oz. anchovies
12 stuffed olives
2 cloves garlic, minced
1/4 cup olive oil
1 tbsp. fresh chopped basil or 1/2 tsp. dried basil
1/4 tsp. chili powder
1/2 cup chopped parsley
1/4 tsp. salt
1/4 tsp. black pepper

Peel and chop tomatoes. Drain and chop anchovies. Slice olives. Cook garlic in olive oil until garlic turns light brown. Add all ingredients to the pan. Simmer for 15 to 20 minutes. Serve over your favorite pasta. Makes 4 servings.

Sicilian Spaghetti

Eggplant is an exotic vegetable to some people, but to the people of the Mediterranean, it is a favorite vegetable, easily grown and easily prepared in a variety of ways.

3 large eggplants
1½ tbsp. extra virgin olive oil
1 16-oz. can crushed tomatoes
½ tsp. oregano
2 tbsp. tomato paste
½ tsp. salt
¼ tsp. pepper
1 lb. ground round
1 large onion, chopped
2 cloves garlic, mashed
8 oz. spaghetti
8 oz. frozen peas
3 oz. cheddar cheese
3 oz. Parmesan cheese
4 tbsp. Italian-style or plain breadcrumbs
Chopped parsley for garnish

Wash eggplant and cut into ⅛-inch slices. Heat oil in a skillet and pan-fry eggplant slices until they are brown on each side. Add tomato, oregano, tomato paste, salt, and pepper and simmer until liquid is reduced by about half. Brown meat and add to tomato mixture. Add onions and garlic and cook for about 10 minutes. Boil spaghetti until tender. Drain. Cook peas until tender. Combine meat with spaghetti, peas, and grated cheeses. Grease a 9-inch round cake pan. Sprinkle breadcrumbs onto bottom and sides of pan. Place 1 slice of eggplant in the center of the pan. Cover the bottom and sides of the dish with eggplant slices. Spoon meat mixture into the pan. Cover with eggplant slices of eggplant and sprinkle with remaining breadcrumbs. Bake uncovered at 350 degrees for about 30 minutes or until golden brown. Let stand for 5 minutes before serving. Sprinkle with chopped parsley. Makes 6 servings.

Pasta Milanese

The late Pete Sclafani, long-time owner of Sclafani's Restaurant on Causeway Boulevard, offered this authentic version of Pasta Milanese. It takes a certain amount of chutzpah, or the Italian equivalent of that trait, to start out as a blacksmith and end up as a successful restaurateur.

Mr. Pete had me laughing out loud as he told the story of how he met his wife, Myrtle. He met Myrtle when he was coming out from under the anesthetic after an operation. He said, "As I woke up, I grabbed for something and caught my wife. Myrtle became my wife, the bookkeeper, bartender, and the Baptist." He continued, "I will never forget her embarrassment when a local preacher came to the restaurant to ask her to be the nurse for a Baptist convention and he found her behind the bar."

Today, Mr. Pete's son, Frank, is the owner and instructor of Sclafani's Cooking School.

1 clove garlic, finely minced
4 green onions, chopped
1 tsp. dried oregano
Pinch of red pepper
Pinch of salt
1/4 cup olive oil
1 stalk or 1/2 cup fresh fennel, chopped
1 tsp. dried parsley or
1 tbsp. fresh parsley, chopped
6 anchovy fillets, chopped
2 tbsp. raisins, chopped
2 cups plum tomatoes, chopped; reserve juice
3 cups water
2 bay leaves
1/2 cup plain breadcrumbs
2 tbsp. olive oil
1 tbsp. brown sugar
1 tbsp. powdered sugar

Sauté garlic, onions, oregano, red pepper, and salt in olive oil. Add fennel, parsley, anchovies, raisins, tomatoes with juice, and water. Simmer for 30 minutes. Add sugars. In a separate pan, toast breadcrumbs in olive oil. Serve sauce over pasta. Sprinkle with toasted breadcrumbs. This is the sauce served over pasta at St. Joseph altars. Milanese sauce can also be served over boiled eggs, boiled fennel, or cauliflower. Makes 6 servings.

Shirley's Pasta Milanese

Shirley says this sauce should just "smile" while simmering. She recommends cooking pork in this gravy, too.

2 large onions, chopped
6 to 8 cloves garlic, minced
1/4 cup olive oil
1 large bunch fennel; remove leaves and reserve for boiling pasta
2 8-oz. cans tomato sauce
5 6-oz. cans tomato paste
6 cups water
1 cup sugar
8 anchovies, minced
1 tsp. oregano
1/4 tsp. cinnamon
1/2 cup Parmesan cheese
1 doz. boiled eggs
Salt and pepper to taste

Sauté onions and garlic in olive oil. Chop fennel stems and add to onions. Continue cooking until fennel is soft. Add remaining ingredients. Simmer over low heat for about 1 hour or to desired consistency. Serve over boiled eggs. Makes 12 servings.

Homemade Pasta

I used to make pasta when my children were little and they always helped. I think they thought it was Play Doh. We loved the homemade pasta but not the mess left in its wake.

2 cups all-purpose flour
3 large eggs

Place flour on a large work surface. Make a well in the center of the flour. Work eggs into the flour until all is incorporated. Knead dough by hand or in the food processor. Let dough rest for 30 minutes. Roll out to 1/8-inch thickness with a rolling pin or put through pasta machine. Cut by hand or with the pasta machine. Let pasta dry by draping over dowel rods suspended between 2 chairs. Makes 1 1/2 pounds pasta. Serves 6.

Aunt Lena's Tomato Gravy

Uncle Charles Culotta shared his mother's recipe for tomato gravy, which his wife, Lena, loved to prepare. Aunt Lena was a gracious hostess and her skills in the kitchen were recognized far and wide. Back in the '40s she was known to have flown *arancini* (rice balls) and *spiedini* (rolled steak) to Hollywood and Las Vegas at the request of celebrities.

3 large onions, chopped
1/2 cup olive oil
5 cloves garlic, minced
10 6-oz. cans tomato paste
3 3/4 pt. water
8 28-oz. cans crushed tomatoes
1 28-oz. can Angela Mia stewed tomatoes
1/3 cup fennel seed
1/3 cup Tex-Joy seasoning
1/3 cup dried basil
1/3 cup black pepper
10 lb. Italian sausage

Fry onions in oil until translucent. Add garlic and cook 5 minutes, stirring constantly. Add remaining ingredients. Simmer 3 hours or until sauce reaches desired consistency. Stir frequently to prevent scorching. Makes 50 servings.

St. Joseph Day Breadcrumbs

In some families these breadcrumbs are called St. Joseph Sawdust. The Millets, Notos, Libertos, and Cascios all make the breadcrumbs this way.

French or Italian bread
Sugar, salt, and pepper to taste

Grate bread. Sift out large pieces. Toast lightly in the oven at 300 degrees. Season with a little white sugar, salt sprinkle and pepper. Sprinkle over pasta in place of grated cheese. Makes 30 servings.

St. Joseph Sweet Gravy

Mary Cascio of Shreveport sent the instructions for preparing this sauce, which can be served with fennel, cauliflower, or boiled eggs.

12 lb. onions, finely chopped
1 qt. olive oil
1 gal. tomato paste
2 gal. plus 2 cups water
Salt, pepper, and sugar to taste

Sauté onions in oil until translucent. Add tomato paste and cook for about 30 minutes, stirring to prevent scorching. Add water, salt, pepper, and sugar. Cover and bring to a boil. Uncover and cook over low heat until sauce reaches desired consistency. Serve over pasta and vegetables. Makes 40 servings.

A Simple Italian Gravy

As simple as this gravy is to make, it is unbelievable that it is so outstanding. This recipe is the specialty of my friend, Vicky Hymel, who has always helped me with my St. Joseph altars. Though Vicki does not sweeten her gravy, my husband's cousin, Rosemary Luke, who made all the gravy for one of my altars, makes a similar gravy and sweetens it with applesauce. Vicky's nephew also varies the recipe by using garlic in place of onions. The following recipe is my version of Vicky's gravy.

4 large onions, chopped fine
½ cup cooking oil or olive oil
4 6-oz cans tomato paste
3 qt. water
Salt and pepper to taste

Sauté onions until clear. Add tomato paste and fry the paste for about 20 minutes. Add water. Season with salt and pepper. Simmer for about 2 hours or until reduced to approximately 2 quarts. Makes 8 servings.

Matilda's Meatballs and Gravy

Patty Amato shared her mom's recipe with me many years ago. It can't be beat!

1 lb. ground chuck
1 tsp. salt
1/4 tsp. black pepper
1/2 cup finely chopped onion
1 clove garlic, minced
1/2 cup Italian-style breadcrumbs
1/4 cup Parmesan cheese
1 egg
1/2 tsp. seasoning blend

Place all ingredients in a bowl and mix well. Shape 8 meatballs. Place in pan and bake at 350 degrees for about 25 minutes or until nicely browned.

Sauce
3 cups finely chopped onion
3 cloves garlic, minced
2 tbsp. olive oil
1 28-oz can tomato sauce
1 tsp. Italian seasoning blend
1/2 tsp. salt
1/4 tsp. black pepper
1 bay leaf
1 tsp. sugar
4 cups water

Sauté onions and garlic in olive oil for 10 minutes. Add remaining ingredients. Place meatballs in sauce. Simmer for 2 hours or until sauce reaches desired consistency. Makes 6 servings.

Eggs in Red Gravy

My mother, who grew up in a family with 8 siblings, told me that chicken and andouille gumbo was often extended by adding boiled eggs to the gumbo. So, why not use boiled eggs for protein in red gravy? This dish was often a Friday night Lenten dish in many Italian households.

8 eggs, hard boiled
Water to boil
1 qt. tomato gravy
1 lb. pasta
½ cup Parmesan cheese, grated

Place eggs in a pot and cover with water. Bring water to a boil then cover pot and immediately turn off heat. Let eggs sit for 15 minutes. Remove shells from eggs and place eggs in tomato gravy. Boil pasta. Serve gravy over pasta, allowing 1 egg per serving. Top with cheese. Makes 8 servings.

Pecan Sauce

This is a great sauce for any vegetable pasta or gnocchi.

2 cloves garlic, mashed
3 tbsp. butter
½ cup olive oil
1 cup pecans
½ cup Parmesan cheese
1 cup heavy cream
1 tsp. chopped fresh basil
¼ tsp. salt
¼ tsp. black pepper
Chicken broth

Sauté garlic in butter and oil mixture. Remove garlic and add pecans. Roast pecans, stirring constantly to keep from burning. Place roasted pecans in a food processor and chop fine. Place pecans in a quart jar or plastic container. Add remaining ingredients. Stir well. Before serving add chicken broth to bring sauce to desired consistency. Makes 4 servings.

Basil-Walnut Pesto

This is wonderful served over hot pasta or on crispy French or Italian bread.

4 cloves garlic
1 cup fresh basil leaves
1 tsp. salt
1/4 cup walnuts or pine nuts
1/3 cup Parmesan cheese
1/3 cup olive oil

Place all ingredients in a food processor. Process 1 minute. Place in jar and refrigerate. Makes 1 cup.

Seafood and Meat

A perusal of Italian cookbooks reveals that the Mediterranean immigrants must have felt very much at home in Louisiana. They settled in an area that was largely Catholic. The climate was similar to that of their homeland. Familiar foods could be grown with ease. All manner of seafood could be fished from the fresh and salt water in the area. Frogs, eels, base, carp, pike, perch, grouper, clams, crabs, shrimp, and octopus were easily accessible.

Seafood-Stuffed Artichoke

Using the seafood plentiful in the New Orleans area, locals have perfected a variety of seafood dishes reminiscent of the old country. In Italy, seafood was readily available since seafaring was one of the country's most popular occupations.

2 artichokes
Water to cover
2 tsp. salt
1 lemon, sliced
½ cup olive oil
⅓ cup onions chopped
2 cloves garlic, minced
4 anchovy fillets, chopped
1 cup raw shrimp, finely chopped
4 oz. fresh or canned crabmeat
½ cups Italian-style breadcrumbs
½ cup chicken stock

Trim off pointed leaf ends of artichokes and cut stems so that the bottom of each artichoke is flat. Place in a deep pot and cover with water. Add salt and lemon slices. Boil until artichokes are tender. Drain. Remove center leaves and spread others apart. Heat oil in pan. Add onions and fry until lightly browned. Add garlic, anchovies, shrimp, and crabmeat. Stir and cook until shrimp have turned pink. Add breadcrumbs and chicken stock. Fill cavities and leaves of artichokes with stuffing. Place artichokes in a deep pot and add 2 inches of water. Cover and cook until leaves can be removed easily. Makes 4 servings.

Codfish Balls

(Crocchetti di Baccala)

Mrs. Frank Monica said that this is a family favorite. In true Italian tradition, her 8 children were named after family members. Anthony was named for Grandfather Monica, Phyllis for Grandmother Fillippa Monica, Anna for Grandmother Navarra, Carl for Uncle Gerald, Frank for his father, Maria Rose for an aunt, and Fano for his Uncle Epifanio. Antoinette, called Anita or Cookie, was the only child not named after a family member.

With such a large family, there were always babies in the house. Once, when she was breastfeeding her baby, Fano asked, "Why do cows have milk?" His mother replied, "Because they eat grass." Fano looked at her quizzically and replied, "You don't eat grass."

One year Mrs. Monica made codfish balls with 50 pounds of potatoes. She had little money for her altar, but she prayed to St. Joseph, "If you want me to have this altar, send me some money." The next day she received a $100 donation.

1 7-oz. can codfish flakes
½ bunch green onions, chopped
¼ bunch parsley, chopped
2 cups mashed potatoes
1 egg
Pepper and salt to taste
1¼ cups breadcrumbs
Oil for frying

Combine all ingredients except breadcrumbs and oil. Mix well and shape into 8 balls or patties. Roll in breadcrumbs and fry in hot oil until lightly browned. Drain and serve hot. Makes 6 servings.

Baccala

Kay Mortillaro of Metairie said, "One of the most popular dishes is baccala, a stinky dried fish. If you can't stand the smell of the fish when you buy it, tie it to the roof of the car to bring it home. Hold your nose to bring it inside. Unwrap it, place it in a pan of cold water, and leave home. Return home every few hours to change the water. Do this for 24 to 48 hours. When ready to cook, it will not smell so bad anymore. Drain. Cut the fish in serving-size pieces. Roll in egg beaten with a little water and seasoned with salt and pepper. Pass it in flour. Fry in olive oil.

Serve hot. You would never believe that this is the same fish that you brought home a couple of days ago. It is very good!"

Ann Biunda of Independence sent this recipe, which is a favorite St. Joseph's Day dish.

2 lb. whole dried codfish
Water to cover
2 cups flour
1 cup water, more or less
3 cups oil for frying

Soak fish in cold tap water overnight. Next morning drain fish. Cover with lukewarm water and let soak another 2 hours. Soak until all water is absorbed. Make a thick paste using flour and water. Use just enough water to make a light batter. Batter the fish. Fry in hot oil.

Sauce
2 medium-sized onions, finely chopped
2 cloves garlic, minced
1/4 cup oil
1/4 cup sweet basil, chopped
2 14-oz. cans chopped tomatoes

Sauté onions and garlic in hot oil. Add remaining ingredients. Simmer until gravy thickens. Serve fish with sauce. Makes 4 to 6 servings.

Fried Eels

3 lb. eels
2/3 cup all-purpose flour
1/2 tsp. salt
1/4 tsp. pepper
1 tsp. rosemary
Olive oil for frying
2 lemons, sliced

Wash eels and remove entrails. Wash eels again and dry with a paper towel. Cut eels crosswise into serving-size pieces. Season flour with salt, pepper, and rosemary. Coat eel with seasoned flour. Heat oil in a skillet then fry eel pieces for about 6 minutes or until golden brown on both sides. Serve with lemon slices. Makes 6 servings.

Baked Redfish with Vegetable Flowers

Josie Messina of Baton Rouge told me that she garnished this baked fish with vegetable flowers when she made it for the St. Joseph altar. The bigger the fish is, the better, if it is for St. Joseph.

1 5-lb. redfish.
½ cup butter, melted
2 cloves garlic, minced
Salt and pepper to taste

Clean fish, leaving the head on but removing eyes. Brush fish with melted butter and rub with garlic. Season with salt and pepper. Place on baking pan. Bake at 350 degrees for about 40 minutes. Serve with tartar sauce and lemon wedges. Makes 6 servings.

Vegetable Flowers
Turnips or potatos
Lemon juice
Carrot slices
Radishes, carrots, small turnips, or small beets, peeled
Cherry tomatoes
Cream cheese, colored
Lemon slices and parsley for garnish

Cut vegetables into flowers for garnishing tray. Cut thin slices of large turnips or potatoes. Dip in lemon juice. Cut flower using a daisy cookie cutter that fits the slice of turnip or potato. Place a small slice of carrot in the center of the daisy. Insert a toothpick so that it holds each "petal" as well as the carrot together.

Roses can be made using radishes, carrots, small turnips or small peeled beets. Beginning at the base of the vegetable, cut thin half-moon wedges out around the vegetable at a 45-degree angle. Remove the wedges; these cuts are the "petals." Cut another row of wedges, placing each petal in this row above and between the petals on the lower row. Continue cutting rows of wedges until you reach the top of the vegetable. Turnip flowers can be colored with vegetable dye.

Make cherry-tomato flowers by cutting 3 broad "v"-shaped petals from the top to the bottom of the tomato. The tomato will now be in 2 halves with "v"-shaped edges. Scoop out pulp and turn petals out. Fill center with colored cream cheese and garnish with parsley or place a pimento-stuffed olive in the center of the tomato.

Cut lemon slices into pointed or scalloped shapes.

Stuffed Redfish "Standing Up"

Frances (Roppollo) Thomassie of Baton Rouge told me how to prepare this dressing, but as with most good cooks, her measurements were given in "abouts" and "little bits." Somehow, I figured this recipe out and it is delicious! Frances said that she baked hers in a large serving platter with the fish standing up.

1 large redfish, 6 to 8 lb. with head on
1 cup celery, finely chopped
1 1/4 cups onion, chopped
3 tbsp. oil
8 cloves garlic, finely minced
1 bunch green onions, finely chopped
1 8-oz. can tomato paste
1 1/2 cups water
1 tbsp. Worcestershire sauce
1/2 cup chopped parsley
2 cups cooked rice
Salt, pepper, and lemon to taste
2 olives

Split fish lengthwise down the belly. Remove entrails and wash fish in cold water. Drain and set aside. Sauté celery and onions in oil for about 10 minutes. Add garlic and green onions. Cook an additional 10 minutes. Add tomato paste, water, Worcestershire sauce, and parsley. Simmer for 30 minutes. Add cooked rice and stir well. Adjust seasonings. Mound stuffing onto platter on which the fish will be baked. Season fish with salt, pepper, and lemon juice and set over stuffing in a "standing" position. Bake at 350 degrees for about 1 hour or until fish flakes from the bone. Garnish and serve. Use olives in place of the eyes. Makes 6 servings.

Baked Stuffed Flounder

Baked stuffed flounder is a popular dish found in restaurants along Louisiana's coastline. As good as this dish is in restaurants, it is in the kitchens of home cooks that this dish reaches perfection!

2 tbsp. chopped onion
1/2 cup chopped green onion
2 ribs celery, finely chopped
4 tbsp. butter
1/2 cup breadcrumbs
1/2 lb. boiled shrimp
1/2 lb. crabmeat
2 tbsp. chopped parsley
1 egg, lightly beaten
1 tsp. salt
1/2 tsp. black pepper
4 medium-size flounders
Lemon wedges

Sauté onions and celery in 2 tablespoons butter. Add breadcrumbs, shrimp, crabmeat, parsley, and egg. Mix well. Add salt and pepper then mix. Split thick side of flounders lengthwise and crosswise. Loosen meat from bone to form a pocket. Brush inside of pocket and outside of fish with remaining butter. Season area with salt and pepper. Divide stuffing among the 4 fish. After they have been stuffed, place fish in greased baking pan. Cover and bake about 25 minutes. Uncover and let brown, baking an additional 5 minutes. Serve with lemon wedges. Makes 4 servings.

Fish Stew

The fish of Italy include scorpion fish, squid, octopus, and other strange creatures not found on most south Louisiana tables. This tasty stew resembles the French court-bouillon.

1 small onion, chopped
2 tbsp. olive oil
6 qt. water
1 lb. large shrimp in shells
2 lb. catfish, skinned and cut into 1-inch cubes; place in cheesecloth bag
8 crabs, cleaned and broken in half

3 tomatoes, peeled and chopped
3 cloves garlic, minced
1/4 tsp. salt
1/4 tsp. black pepper
2 lemon slices
Hot sauce to taste

Sauté onion in olive oil. Add water, seafood, tomatoes, garlic, salt, pepper, and lemon. Bring to a boil. Simmer slowly until seafood is cooked, approximately 8 minutes. Adjust seasoning with salt, pepper, and hot sauce. Makes 12 servings.

Stuffed Crabs

Shirley Dauzat of Baton Rouge could not give me her recipes because she doesn't cook with recipes. Instead she orally shared her secrets to her favorite dishes. She suggests adding chopped mint leaves to meatballs and topping stuffed crabs with tomato gravy seasoned with basil. Here is my version of stuffed crabs based on my conversation with her many years ago. This stuffing also makes very good crab cakes.

1/2 cup olive oil
1 1/2 cups onion, finely chopped
3/4 cup celery, finely chopped
6 green onions, finely chopped
4 cloves garlic, finely minced
2 lb. crabmeat
4 slices bread, soaked in water and squeezed
2 eggs
1/2 tsp. cayenne pepper
1/4 tsp. black pepper
1 1/2 tsp. salt
1/4 tsp. ground bay leaves
1/4 tsp. thyme
Water
8 clean crab shells
(Boiling shells for 20 minutes with 2 tsp. baking soda makes for easy cleaning)

Sauté onions, celery, green onions, and garlic in olive oil for 10 minutes. Add crabmeat, bread, eggs, and seasonings. Mix well. Add a little water until mixture is stiff. Adjust seasonings to taste. Pile stuffing into crab shells. Cover with your favorite tomato gravy seasoned with basil and bake for 20 minutes. Makes 8 servings.

Shirley's Stuffed Hard Shell Crabs

4 crabs
1 egg
1/2 cup Parmesan cheese
1/2 cup Italian-style breadcrumbs
1 clove garlic, minced
1/4 tsp. salt
1/8 tsp. black pepper
2 green onions, chopped

Scald crabs. Remove large outer shell, claws, fingers, and other inedible parts. Mix egg, cheese, breadcrumbs, garlic, salt, pepper, and green onions. Stuff this mixture in cavity of crab bodies. Fry in hot oil. Add to your favorite tomato gravy and simmer for 30 minutes. Makes 4 servings.

Baked Oysters

1 pt. raw oysters, drained
3 tbsp. olive oil
1 tsp. Italian seasoning blend
1 tsp. Tabasco
1 lemon

Pat oysters dry with paper towel. Season with olive oil, seasoning blend, Tabasco, and lemon juice. Bake at 350 degrees until edges of oysters curl. Serve hot with French bread. Makes 4 servings.

Barbequed Shrimp

1 lb. butter or margarine
1 tbsp. Italian seasoning blend
1/4 tsp. cayenne pepper
2 tsp. salt
1 tsp. liquid crab boil
2 lb. large shrimp, heads on

Melt butter in a large baking pan. Mix in seasonings. Place shrimp in pan and stir. Bake at 350 degrees until shrimp turn pink. Serve with hot French or Italian bread. Makes 4 servings.

Shrimp Scampi

2 tbsp. butter
2 green onions, minced
16 large shrimp
½ tsp. salt
½ tsp. pepper
½ cup dry vermouth
2 threads saffron
1 cup heavy cream or half and half
1 tbsp. lemon juice

Melt butter in a skillet. Add green onions and shrimp; cook until shrimp turn pink. Add salt, pepper, and vermouth. Stir to deglaze pan. Cook about 8 minutes, then remove shrimp from pan. Add saffron and simmer for 2 minutes. Add cream and simmer until thickened. Add lemon juice and cook 2 additional minutes. Place shrimp in sauce. Adjust seasoning to taste. Serve with hot crusty bread. Makes 2 servings.

Lobsters for St. Joseph

Beautiful lobsters are often found on altars. One year the Bosco altar in Luling featured huge Maine lobsters that a friend had flown in for the occasion. Remember, "Nothing is too good for St. Joseph!"

4 gal. water
4 tbsp. Old Bay seasoning
1 lemon
1 large onion
2 ribs celery
2 lobsters

Bring water, seasoning, lemon, and vegetables to a boil. Add lobsters. Cook lobsters for 3 to 5 minutes after the water again reaches a boil. Do not overcook; overcooked lobsters will be tough. Serve with hot, crusty Italian bread and melted butter mixed with fresh lemon juice for a tasty meal. Makes 2 lobsters.

Homemade Seasoning

If Old Bay seasoning is not available, this seasoning makes a great substitute to season boiled lobsters.

3/4 cup salt
1 tsp. cloves
1 tbsp. garlic powder
1 tsp. coriander
4 bay leaves or 2 tsp. powdered bay leaves
2 tsp. mustard seed
1 tsp. allspice
2 tsp. celery seed

Combine all ingredients. Mix and store in covered jar. Use in place of Old Bay seasoning to season water.

Stuffed Squid

Today, that which seemed exotic and unattainable a few years ago is available in specialty stores around the nation. The South is no different. Perhaps this change has occurred because air travel is so widely used and children, as well as adults, have seen much more of the world than people of previous decades. Do your children talk of sushi as you did of crawfish in your youth? They seem to be much more adventuresome than my generation.

1 2-lb. squid
1 large onion, chopped
2 cloves garlic
3 tbsp. olive oil
2 tbsp. fresh parsley, chopped
8 black olives, pitted
4 tbsp. plain breadcrumbs
2 tbsp. Parmesan cheese
1/2 tsp. oregano
4 fresh tomatoes, peeled, seeded, and chopped
1 tbsp. capers
1/2 tsp. salt
1 cup water

Clean the squid by removing the eyes, beak, fin, and sac. Wash until squid turns white. Remove tentacles and chop. Set aside.

Sauté onion, garlic, olives, and parsley in olive oil until onions turn brown. Add tentacles and cook for 5 minutes. Add breadcrumbs, cheese, and oregano. Stuff body and secure with toothpicks. Place in pan and add tomatoes, capers, and salt. Add water and bring to a boil. Reduce heat and simmer for about 30 minutes. Add more water if additional liquid is needed during cooking time. Makes 6 servings.

Tortellini Soup

2 eggs
2 egg whites
3 tbsp. olive oil
2 1/4 tsp. salt
3 cups flour
2 qt. chicken broth

Filling
2 1/2 cups boneless chicken, finely chopped
1/4 cup grated Parmesan cheese
1/8 tsp. pepper
2 egg yolks

Place eggs, egg whites, oil, and 2 teaspoons salt in a bowl. Beat on low for 2 minutes. Gradually add flour. Knead with dough hook to make stiff dough. Wrap dough in wax paper and set aside. Combine filling ingredients and set aside. Divide dough into 4 pieces. Roll each piece into a large round as thin as possible. Cut into 30 2-inch rounds, making approximately 90 rounds. For each tortellini, place about 1 teaspoon chicken filling in center of round. Moisten edges with water. Fold in half, making sure the top edge comes just short of the bottom edge. Seal edges. Shape into rings by gently forming the tortellini around your finger. Press tips together. Bring broth to a boil. Drop tortellini in broth and cook about 15 minutes or until tortellini is tender. Makes 10 servings.

Roasted Garlic Chicken

There is nothing like the sweet roasted aroma of garlic! Use with chicken or fish to give sweet pungency to mild-flavored meats.

1 large head garlic
2 tbsp. olive oil
3 boneless, skinless chicken breast cut in strips
1 tsp. salt
1/4 tsp. black pepper
Olive oil for frying
1/2 lb. fresh green beans, blanched
3 cups chopped fresh tomatoes with juice
1 lb. narrow egg noodles, cooked
1/4 cup chopped, fresh basil
1/2 cup Kalamata olives, pitted and coarsely chopped

Cut about 1/2 inch off the garlic head, exposing the meat in all cloves. Drizzle with 2 tablespoons olive oil. Wrap in aluminum foil and bake until garlic is soft, about 25 to 30 minutes. Peel garlic after cooling. Season chicken with salt and pepper. Fry in hot olive oil until lightly browned. Place chicken, garlic, green beans, tomato, noodles, and basil in a large casserole dish. Season with additional salt and pepper and chopped olives. Toss and serve. Makes 8 servings.

Italian Roasted Chicken

This chicken dish can be baked, barbecued, or broiled. It is a favorite Sunday dinner.

1 chicken, a fryer cut into serving-size pieces
3 tbsp. olive oil
1 tsp. salt
1/2 tsp. black pepper
1/2 tsp. powdered garlic
1 tsp. Italian seasoning blend

Rub chicken with olive oil and seasonings. Place on broiler pan. Cook 10 minutes or longer on each side. Broiling and baking time will depend on the size of the chicken. Makes 4 to 6 servings.

Italian Chicken

1 chicken
½ cup butter, melted
1 tsp. salt
½ tsp. black pepper
2 cups Italian-style breadcrumbs

Be sure to buy a fryer and not a hen for cooking. A fryer is a young chicken that is tender when cooked in about 1 hour. Cut chicken in serving-size pieces. Roll each chicken piece in melted butter and season with salt and pepper. Roll chicken in breadcrumbs. Bake in preheated oven at 350 degrees for 45 minutes or until tender. Makes 6 servings.

Chicken Livers to Die For

Invariably, when talking with descendents of the early immigrants, the topic of chickens arises. Farms and chickens, along with goats and cows, go together. No wonder the early immigrants did not feel deprived. They could enjoy good food because they could grow it or catch it in the farmyard.

20 slices bacon
20 fresh chicken livers
½ tsp. powdered bay leaves
1 tsp. salt
¼ tsp. black pepper or crushed red pepper
1 large onion, sliced
1 green bell pepper, sliced
½ cup water

Fry bacon until crisp. Remove meat from skillet. Brown chicken livers in bacon grease. Drain off all but 2 tablespoons grease. Add bacon, powdered bay leaves, salt, pepper, onion, bell pepper, and water. Cover and cook on low for about 15 minutes. Serve with polenta. Makes 6 servings.

Liver and Onions

1 lb. calf liver
1 cup flour
1 tsp. salt
1/2 tsp. black pepper
3 large onions, chopped
2 tbsp. butter
3 tbsp. olive oil
1 tbsp. chopped parsley

Remove the skin around the liver then cut liver into thin strips. Season with salt and pepper and coat with flour. Heat butter and 1 tablespoon oil in skillet, add onions, and cook until lightly browned. Reserve onions. Add 2 tablespoons oil to skillet in which onions were cooked. Turn heat to high, add liver, and cook for 2 minutes or until liver is browned. Return onions to pan and cook for additional 2 minutes. Sprinkle with parsley. Season with additional salt and pepper or hot sauce if desired. Makes 6 servings.

Roasted Squab

"Squab" is a fancy name for the birds that were killed on the farms and found themselves in the stew pots or the mud ovens of every farm family.

6 birds
3 tbsp. olive oil
1/2 tsp. salt
1/4 tsp. black pepper
2 cloves garlic, smashed

Dip the birds in hot water. Remove feathers. Split down back and remove entrails. Season birds by rubbing them with olive oil, salt, pepper, and garlic. Place birds in a heavy roasting pan. Bake at 350 degrees for about 35 minutes or until birds are tender and brown. Serve with buttered noodles. Makes 6 servings.

Italian Rabbit Roast

1 fresh 3-lb. rabbit, not wild
2 tbsp. butter, melted
1 tsp. salt
½ tsp. black pepper
1 large onion
1 rib celery
1 long "branch" rosemary
2 tbsp. white wine
1 cup water

Season rabbit with butter, salt, and pepper. Place ½ onion, celery, and rosemary inside rabbit body. Place rabbit in roasting pan. Slice remaining onion and spread over rabbit. Bake at 350 degrees for about 1 hour or until rabbit is well browned and meat thermometer reads 160 degrees. Remove rabbit from pan. Pour white wine and water into pan, stirring well to dissolve brown particles from the bottom of pan. Season with salt and pepper. Simmer 5 minutes to reduce liquid by ¼ to make gravy. Makes 6 servings.

Italian Sausage with Onions and Peppers

1 lb. mild Italian sausage
1 green bell pepper, sliced and seeds removed
1 medium onion, sliced
¼ tsp. salt
¼ tsp. black pepper
¼ cup water

Prick sausage casing with a fork. Brown sausage in a hot skillet. Reduce heat and cook until sausage is slightly done. Drain most of the grease, leaving about 2 tablespoons in the pan. Add onions and peppers and fry until vegetables are lightly browned and soft. Add water to deglaze the pan then add salt, pepper, and water. Cover and cook sausage and vegetables an additional 5 minutes. Serve on Italian bread or over pasta. Makes 6 servings.

Uncle Neutsie Morrell's Italian Sausage

Uncle Neutsie, formerly a butcher in Beaumont, Texas, was trained in this trade by his mother, Rosita Culotta. Apparently he was proud of this recipe because according to his nephew, Charles Culota, Uncle Neutsie shared it with everyone.

50 lb. lean pork butt
12 oz. salt
8 oz. black peppper
6 oz. fennel seed
Casings for sausage

Cube and season meat then refrigerate overnight. Grind coarsely with a meat grinder and stuff into casings or make patties. Freeze or cook immediately. Great in tomato gravy! Makes 50 pounds of sausage.

Osso Buco

4 lb. beef or veal shanks cut in 2-inch pieces
1/4 cup all-purpose flour
2 tbsp. olive oil
1/4 cup butter, melted
2 slices bacon, diced
3 large onions, chopped
3 cloves garlic, minced
3 bay leaves or 1 tsp. bay leaf powder
1 tsp. dried rosemary
1 tsp. pepper, your choice
3/4 cup dry white or red wine
1 carrot, grated
4 ribs celery
1/4 cup chopped parsley
2 large tomatoes, chopped
1 cup crushed tomatoes
2 tbsp. tomato paste
1/2 to 1 cup warm water

Sprinkle shanks with flour. Mix oil, butter, and bacon in skillet. Brown shanks and remove from pan. Add onions and cook until lightly browned. Add remaining ingredients. Stir to deglaze bottom of pan. Return shanks to pan. Cover and simmer over low heat until meat is tender and falling from bone. If necessary, add more water during cooking. Makes 4 to 6 servings.

Ragout of Beef, Pork Knuckles, and Cabbage

There was no written recipe for this dish, which is essentially a stew. I concocted the following recipe from the bits and pieces of my memory of an interview with several ladies many years ago. The ingredients, especially cabbage, are traditional ones that were easily grown on country farms and could be used by the family or marketed in the French Quarter.

1 3-lb. chuck roast
2 oz. salt meat
1 medium-size cabbage
2 lb. pork knuckles, cracked
2 cups water
1/2 cup olive oil
1/2 cup butter
2 cloves garlic, mashed
3 large onions, chopped
1/2 cup mushrooms, chopped
1 oz. chicken livers
1 large tomato, peeled and chopped
2 tsp. salt
1/2 tsp. black pepper
3 cups hot water or beef broth

Cut roast into 1-inch cubes and chop salt meat into very small pieces. Core cabbage and chop leaves. Set these ingredients aside. Place pork roast and pork knuckles in a large pot and cover with water. Boil for about 30 minutes then drain and discard water. Place olive oil, butter, salt meat, garlic, and onions in a large soup pot. Add meat and remaining ingredients and bring to a slow boil. Simmer until meat is tender. Add chopped cabbage and continue cooking until cabbage is limp. Season with hot sauce if desired. Makes 8 servings.

Tripe Soup

The Italians probably used busecca, or tripe soup, as a hangover remedy just as the Mexicans use menudo.

2 large onions, finely chopped
½ tsp. sage
3 tbsp. lard
2 tbsp. butter
2 lb. tripe, cut into small pieces
1 large carrot, peeled and diced
2 ribs celery
1 qt. vegetable or chicken broth
6 slices bread, day old

Sauté onions and sage in lard and butter. Wilt the onions. Add tripe and cook for approximately 8 minutes. Add carrot, celery, and broth. Simmer until tripe is tender, approximately 3 hours. Add additional broth if needed. Serve in a soup plate over a slice of bread. Makes 4 servings.

Meatball Soup

My husband says, "When you hava the meataballs, you gotta hava the pasta"—even if the meatballs are in a soup.

1 lb. ground beef
1 tsp. salt
¼ tsp. black pepper
2 tbsp. chopped onion
1 tbsp. chopped parsley
½ cup Italian-style breadcrumbs
1 egg
⅓ cup Parmesan cheese
2 qt. beef stock
8 oz. noodles or vermicelli

Mix beef, salt, pepper, onion, parsley, breadcrumbs, egg, and cheese together. Shape into small 1-inch meatballs. Brown in a 350-degree oven. Bring stock to a boil. Add browned meatballs and cook about 10 minutes. Add pasta or vermicelli. Cook until tender and season with additional salt and pepper if desired. Serve with additional cheese. Makes 6 servings.

Rollatini

Mrs. Joseph Biundo of Independence sent this recipe for rollatini. Though generally St. Joseph's Day feasts do not offer meat, if you choose to break with tradition, this would be a good dish to serve.

16 pieces scaloppini of veal, about 4 inches by 6 inches
8 slices ham, about 1/4-inch thick
2 lb. mozzarella or Gruyere cheese, sliced
1 bunch green onions, chopped
1/4 cup chopped parsley
1 tsp. salt
1/2 tsp. black pepper
2 cups flour
1/3 cup olive oil
1/4 cup butter
4 cloves garlic, minced
1 cup white wine
1/2 lb. fresh or canned mushrooms, sliced
1/2 cup water

Lay veal scaloppini flat. Season with salt and pepper. Cut ham slices in half then top veal with 1 slice of ham and 1 slice of cheese. Mix green onions and parsley and place 1 teaspoon of this mixture on cheese. Season with salt and pepper. Roll veal and secure with a toothpick. Dip veal rolls in flour. Heat olive oil and butter in a heavy skillet. Add garlic and sauté until garlic is browned. Discard garlic but retain garlic-flavored oil. Brown veal rolls on all sides. Add wine. Cover and cook on low for approximately 1/2 hour, turning frequently. Remove meat and add mushrooms. Add water to deglaze pan. Cook mushrooms for 10 minutes. Makes 8 servings.

Braciolone

Angelina Mitchell prepared this dish for the Nicholls State University faculty meeting, which I attended as an instructor at the university many years ago.

1/4 cup butter
1 3-lb. flank steak, trimmed
1/2 cup chopped ham
1 hard-boiled egg, chopped
2 tbsp. grated Parmesan cheese
1 tsp. salt
1/4 tsp. black pepper
1/2 cup olive oil

Spread butter on steak. Spread ham, egg, and cheese over steak. Season with salt and pepper. Roll steak and tie with string in several places. Fry in oil until brown, approximately 15 minutes. Place in baking pan.

Sauce
1 large onion, chopped
1 bell pepper, seeded and chopped
1/4 cup olive oil
1 tsp. basil
1 28-oz. can tomato sauce
1 cup water

Sauté onion and bell pepper in hot oil for 10 minutes. Add remaining ingredients. Pour sauce over steak. Cover and bake at 350 degrees for 2 hours. Makes 8 servings.

Spiedini

Salvatore and Rosa (Passarella) Culotta came to the United States from Palermo around the turn of the century. Supposedly one of the 8 Culotta children was born on the boat coming over. In America, the family continued to practice their Old World customs. It seems that at the time there was at least one nun or priest in every Italian family. Sadie became a Dominican nun while Charles's son and Neutsie's son each became a priest. Others carried on the culinary tradition in the family. Rosita cooked the way her mother taught her. She cooked cauliflower and beans with pasta, tomato gravy with eggs, and when she had the time and the money, she cooked her beloved spiedini.

Here is my favorite entree for an Italian dinner. Serve Sebastini Barbera with this tasty main dish.

4 slices bacon
1/4 cup olive oil
1/4 cup onion, minced
1/2 cup celery, finely chopped
2 cloves garlic, finely minced
1 tsp. dried oregano
1 3/4 cups breadcrumbs made from stale hamburger buns
1/4 cup Parmesan cheese
Salt and pepper to taste
1 1/2-lb. eye of the round roast, chilled and sliced very thin by the butcher

Basting Sauce
1/2 cup lemon juice
1/2 cup olive oil
1 tbsp. Worcestershire sauce

Cook bacon in a skillet until very crisp. Remove bacon and crumble. Discard all but 2 tablespoons grease. Add olive oil. Place onions, celery, and garlic in oil and sauté until onion is lightly browned. Add remaining ingredients, reserving 3/4 cup of breadcrumbs, and mix well. Season with salt and pepper. Place 1 teaspoon of filling on each slice of meat. Fold 2 sides to the center and roll from one of the unfolded sides. Place 5 such rolls on a skewer. Prepare the basting sauce. Dip skewered beef rolls into sauce. Roll in remaining breadcrumb mixture. Broil 5 minutes on each side or until lightly browned. Makes 6 servings.

Pork Chop Milanese

4 center-cut pork chops, boneless
4 oz. mozzarella cheese
½ tsp. salt
¼ tsp. black pepper
1 egg, beaten
2 cups plain or Italian-style breadcrumbs
¼ cup butter

Pound chops flat with a mallet. Place cheese on chop and season with salt and pepper. Fold chops in half to cover cheese. Dip into egg then in breadcrumbs. Melt butter in a pan. Place chops in melted butter. Fry on each side using additional butter if necessary. Makes 4 servings.

Steak with Merlot Sauce

1 large onion, finely chopped
¾ cup beef broth
¾ cup Merlot or other dry red wine
1 tbsp. chopped fresh rosemary
½ tsp. salt
¼ cup Italian seasoning
3 cloves garlic, smashed
1 1-lb. flank steak
2 tbsp. olive oil
1 tbsp. tomato paste
2 tsp. Dijon mustard

Place onion, beef broth, wine, rosemary, salt, Italian seasoning, and garlic in a heavy-duty freezer bag. Place steak in bag and marinate in refrigerator for about 30 minutes. Remove from marinade and drizzle olive oil on steak. Cook steak on grill or in broiler to desired temperature. Combine marinade with tomato paste and mustard in a small skillet. Stir with a whisk until smooth. Simmer for about 6 minutes. Slice steak across the grain. Pour sauce over steak. Makes 6 servings.

Veal Parmesan

4 pieces veal, about 6 oz. each
1 cup flour
1/2 tsp. salt
1/4 tsp. black pepper
1 egg
1 tbsp. water
1 cup plain breadcrumbs
1/4 cup oil
2 tbsp. butter
8 oz. mozzarella
1/4 cup Parmesan cheese
1 tbsp. oil, extra

Remove membrane from edges of veal. Pound to tenderize and flatten. Season flour with salt and pepper. Dip veal in egg wash made by beating eggs and water together. Dip veal in flour and breadcrumbs. Heat oil and butter together. Cook veal until tender and golden brown on both sides. Place in ovenproof dish and top with cheese and sauce.

Tomato sauce
1 small onion, chopped
1 rib celery
1 red bell pepper
1 clove garlic, mashed
1 tbsp. olive oil
2 cups whole tomatoes
1 tbsp. parsley, chopped
1/2 tsp. dried basil
2 tsp. sugar
1 tbsp. tomato paste
1 1/2 cups water
1 chicken bouillon cube
1/2 tsp. salt
1/4 tsp. black pepper

Place chopped onion, celery, pepper, and garlic in hot oil used to cook veal. Add remaining ingredients, bring to a boil, and simmer for about 30 minutes. Place sauce over veal and sprinkle with remaining breadcrumbs. Drizzle with olive oil and bake at 350 degrees for 30 minutes. Makes 4 servings.

Horsemeat

Horsemeat has never been looked upon with favor in the United States as a meat for human consumption. However, it is commercially available throughout Europe, and it is often served in place of beef. Used for braising and stewing, it can be cooked in the same manner as beef. Despite the American distaste for this meat, I am sure that sometimes in the Old West horsemeat might have been used to stave off hunger. But the cowboys rarely told.

I offer this information because horsemeat has an interesting place in Italian history. In the Piedmont, a region in northwest Italy, donkey is considered a delicacy. Legend has it that in the Middle Ages a great number of men and horses were killed in battle. The horsemeat was given to the people of Verona, who had been starving because of crop failures. It was under these unfortunate circumstances that the people of Italy discovered that this meat is quite tasty and easy to cook.

Perhaps it is because of our relationships with particular animals that we form attitudes of distaste for the consumption of these creatures. Did you really want a recipe for horsemeat stew?

Unusual Pastries and Desserts

Almond Biscotti

My daughter Angela, a pastry chef, says that biscotti means "twice baked"; therefore, these biscotti are true to the technical definition. Though most of the "little Italian ladies" called at least some of their cookies biscotti, here is the only biscotti in the book that is true to definition. These are the dip-in-your-wine-or-coffee biscotti.

½ cup butter
1 cup granulated sugar
2 tsp. almond flavoring or 3 drops almond oil
3 eggs
3 cups flour
3 tsp. baking powder
¾ tsp. salt
1 cup toasted almonds, finely chopped

Cream butter, sugar, and almond flavoring together. Add eggs 1 at a time, beating well after each addition. Sift flour, baking powder, and salt together. Add to mixture. Stir in almonds. Shape dough into a long loaf about 2 inches in diameter. Bake at 350 degrees for about 25 minutes. Let rest for 20 minutes. With a serrated knife cut loaf into 1-inch slices. Place on cookie sheet and bake 10 additional minutes at 350 degrees. Makes 24 slices.

Variation
Use vanilla in place of almond flavoring and pecans or pistachios in place of almonds.

Almond Cake

4 large eggs
1/3 cup sugar
1 tsp. grated lemon rind
1/3 cup plain flour
1/4 cup corn flour
1/4 cup ground almonds
1 oz. butter
8 oz. red currant jelly

Combine eggs, sugar, and lemon rind in a small bowl. Using an electric mixer, beat on high speed until mixture is thick and frothy and reaches top of bowl. Sift plain flour. Gently fold in sifted flour, corn flour, and ground almonds. Fold in melted butter. Pour mixture into greased and floured 8-inch cake pan. Bake in 325-degree oven for 35 minutes or until cake is done. Turn out on wire rack to cool. Let cake stand overnight.

Cut cake into 3 horizontal layers. Place 1 layer on oven tray and spread with jelly. Top first layer with another layer of cake, spread with jelly, and top with final layer. Reserve extra jelly.

Topping
2 cup ground almonds
1/3 cup sugar
6 large eggs, separated
5 tbsp. rum
1/4 cup flaked almonds

Combine ground almonds and sugar. Mix together egg yolks and rum. Gradually stir into ground-almond mixture. Mix well. Remove 1/3 of this mixture and reserve. Add 1 tablespoon unbeaten egg white to remaining mixture. Mix well. Spread this mixture around sides and top of cake. Topping should be thicker on top of cake than on sides. If mixture is hard to spread, add a little more egg white.

To the remaining almond mixture, add 2 tablespoons unbeaten egg white. Place mixture in piping bag with fitted fluted tube. Decorate top with zig-zag pattern and create small rosettes around the edge. Bake cake in 425-degree oven for 8 to 10 minutes or until sides of cake turn white and rosettes are slightly brown. Remove from oven immediately. Melt remaining currant jelly in pan. Spoon jelly between zig-zag design. Let cake cool 10 minutes then spread leftover jelly on sides and coat with flaked almonds. Allow cake to cool completely before cutting. Makes 8 to 10 servings.

Wedding White Cake

Almond is the flavor of choice for wedding cakes. Many an Italian mother has prayed fervently to "Jesus, Mary, and Joseph" on behalf of her daughter's search for a proper mate. And there is never an Italian wedding without Jordan almonds. Here is an easy "from scratch" recipe from the days before cake mixes.

2½ cups cake flour, sifted
1⅔ cups sugar
⅔ cup Crisco shortening
1 tsp. salt
¾ cup milk
4½ tsp. baking powder
5 egg whites
½ cup milk
1½ tsp. almond flavoring

Place first 5 ingredients in a large mixing bowl and, using an electric mixer, mix on medium speed for 2 minutes. Stir in baking powder. Add egg whites, milk, and almond flavoring. Mix on high for about 3 minutes or until ingredients are well blended and batter is light and fluffy. Pour batter into 2 8-inch pans that have been greased and floured. Bake at 350 degrees for 30 minutes or until top of cake springs back when touched lightly. Remove from oven and cool.

Frosting
1 1-lb. box powdered sugar
2 tsp. almond flavoring
½ cup Crisco shortening
¼ cup water

Beat all frosting ingredients together until light and fluffy. Spread frosting on both cake layers. Stack layers and frost sides and top of cake. Garnish or decorate as desired. Makes 8 to 10 servings.

Amaretti

4 oz. ground almonds
1 cup sugar
2 large egg whites
½ tsp. vanilla
2 tsp. almond flavoring
Blanched almonds for decorating

Combine ground almonds, sugar, unbeaten egg whites, vanilla, and almond flavoring. Mix well. Using an electric mixer, beat mixture on medium for 3 minutes. Let set for 5 minutes. Spoon mixture into piping bag and pipe onto lightly greased baking sheets that have been dusted with flour. Place an almond atop each cookie. Bake at 350 degrees for about 12 minutes. Makes 20 cookies.

Anise Drops

(Biscotti alla Anise)

Theresa Gennussa's parents came to New Orleans from Italy as a young married couple in January 1895. In February the first of their 12 children was born. Six years later, there was a yellow fever epidemic. Mrs. Gennussa prayed that if her family were spared, she would have a St. Joseph altar. Her altars became an annual affair and were known throughout the area.

When the family lived in the Irish Channel, they kept a goat and several chickens. The goat provided the family with milk and cheese, and the chickens provided eggs, which Mrs. Gennussa used in her St. Joseph's Day recipes. Here is the recipe for one of her favorite pastries.

5 "yard" eggs
1 lb. powdered sugar
2 cups all-purpose flour
4 drops anise oil
Nonpareils

Beat eggs well with an electric mixer. Add sugar a little at a time and beat well after each addition. Add flour and anise oil and beat until thoroughly incorporated. Drop dough onto cookie sheet from a teaspoon. Dampen your finger with a little water, dip in nonpareils, then lightly touch your finger to the top of the cookie. Allow about 1 inch between cookies so that they can spread. Let stand 12 hours in a cool place. Do not skip this step. Bake at 300 degrees for about 8 minutes. Do not let cookies brown. Not enough cookie sheets? Drop batter onto parchment paper. Makes about 50 cookies.

Anise Cookies

Georgette Cornelius gave me this recipe, which she got from her husband's sister, Rose (Joseph) Gembrone. The Zito family of Baton Rouge makes a similar cookie.

12 cups all-purpose flour
3 cups sugar
15 tsp. baking powder
1 lb. butter or margarine
4 tbsp. anise seeds
4 cup milk, more or less

Sift dry ingredients together. Cut in butter with a pastry blender or with fingers until mixture is mealy. Add anise seeds and enough milk to make a soft dough. Form into balls, ovals, or animal shapes using a generous tablespoon of dough for each. Bake at 350 degrees for about 12 minutes or until cookies are light brown.

Glaze
2 lb. powdered sugar
1/4 cup water
2 drops anise oil or 4 tsp. anise flavoring

Mix 2 pounds powdered sugar with enough water to make a soft icing. Flavor with anise oil or anise flavoring. Color as you like. Frost cookies by dipping the tops of the cookies into the glaze or by drizzling several brightly colored frostings over the cookies. Makes about 100 cookies.

Gina's Wonderful Anise Cookies

Leah Gros Arrigo and Gina Arrigo Wilson, my daughter-in-law, make these melt-in-your-mouth anise cookies for holiday dinners. Every year we look forward to her contribution to our festive table.

6 cups all-purpose flour
2 cups sugar
3 tbsp. baking powder
Pinch of salt
1 cup Crisco shortening
1/4 cup margarine or butter
2 eggs
1 oz. anise extract
2 tbsp. water
1/2 cup milk

Sift dry ingredients together. Add Crisco and butter. Mix until flaky. Make a well in the center of dough and add eggs, anise extract, water, and milk. Mix and knead dough. Roll in balls and place on greased cookie sheet. Bake at 350 degrees for 22 minutes.

Icing
2 cans prepared vanilla frosting
1 lb. powdered sugar
1 oz. anise extract

Mix all ingredients well in a microwave-safe dish. Microwave for 2 minutes. Drop cookies in icing. Place on a wire rack to dry. Makes about 60 cookies.

Anise Caps

My mother, Lelia Faucheux Tregre, gave me this recipe many years ago. She said that Haydel's Bakery featured this recipe on a local food television show back in the '60s. As a child I would enjoy these cookies, which my mother bought as a special treat for me during our shopping trips to New Orleans.

1 cup sugar
2 eggs
1 1/2 cups all-purpose flour
3 drops anise oil
Nonpareils

Heat sugar and eggs in a double boiler to 115 or 120 degrees. Remove from heat. Beat eggs and sugar with electric mixer on high speed for 10 minutes. Sift flour. Fold in flour and anise oil with a rubber spatula. Do not overmix. Place batter in a pastry bag and squeeze out into quarter-sized rounds onto parchment or lightly greased cookie sheet. Dampen finger with water and dip in nonpareils then touch finger lightly to the top of the cookie. Repeat for each cookie. Let cookies dry overnight so that they form a crust on top. Do not skip this step. Bake at 375 degrees for 8 to 20 minutes. Makes about 24 cookies.

Vanilla Drops

Anna Misura of Baton Rouge said that these are called "savaahtah." I could not find an Italian name for them, but vanilla in Italian is *vaniglia* and pronounced "vah-e-nee-lyah." That's close, huh?

1½ cups butter
6 eggs
1½ cups sugar
1 tsp. vanilla
4 cups flour, or more
½ cup raisins

Beat together butter, eggs, and sugar. Add vanilla and enough flour to make a soft dough. Dough should be a little softer than biscuit dough. Drop by teaspoons onto a greased baking sheet. Place 1 raisin in the center of each cookie. Bake at 350 degrees for about 12 minutes or until lightly browned. Makes 4 dozen.

Spiced Cookies

These cookies, a recipe from Gail Bosco, are called *Biscotti di Cannella* by some. Gail, of French and German heritage, is from the German Coast of Louisiana. Her progenitor Alovon Grainier fled Martigne, France, at the time of the French Revolution. Despite her strong French background, Gail has embraced her husband's Italian heritage, and the names of her children attest to this: Jeno, Joey, and, oops, Ricky.

5 lb. or 20 cups flour
5 tbsp. baking powder
3 cups shortening or butter
4 cups sugar
6 eggs, lightly beaten
¼ tsp. anise oil
6 tbsp. cinnamon (yes, that's right)
6 tbsp. allspice
1 13-oz. can milk
13 oz. water

Sift flour and baking powder together. Cut in shortening with fingers or pastry blender. Add remaining ingredients and mix well. Shape dough into 1-inch balls. Bake at 375 degrees for 15 minutes or until cookie is very dry. Makes 20 dozen cookies.

Biscotti di Grugilena

Here is Lena Boudreaux's recipe for seed "cakes."

8 cups all-purpose flour
1 tbsp. baking powder
2 cups sugar
1 tsp. salt
4 cups shortening
2 eggs
1 cup milk, more or less
1 cup sesame seeds

Mix flour, baking powder, sugar, and salt. Blend shortening into flour with electric mixer until mixture is mealy. Beat eggs with milk. Add eggs to flour mixture to make a soft dough. Knead until smooth. Roll into long sausage-like shapes about 1 inch in diameter. Brush with additional milk then roll in seeds. Place on greased cookie sheet and bake for 20 minutes at 350 degrees. Makes 175 cookies.

Sesame Seed Cookies

Mrs. Jack Pizzalota gave me a recipe for these cookies before she died, and this is her recipe with a few minor changes. She said the secret to good seed cookies is to bake them until they are very dry. Lena LaCroix explained that the best way to stick the seeds to the dough is to brush the dough with milk before rolling it in the seeds.

1 cup butter or Crisco shortening
6 cups sugar
5 eggs
1½ tsp. vanilla
5 lb. all-purpose flour
5 tbsp. baking powder
½ tsp. salt
1 cup milk
2 lb. sesame seeds

Beat butter with sugar and eggs until light and fluffy. Sift together flour, baking powder, and salt. Mix in remaining ingredients except seeds. Knead lightly. Shape into1-inch snakelike forms. Roll shaped dough in milk or brush surface with milk then roll in seeds. Cut in 1-inch pieces. Place on a greased cookie sheet and bake at 375 degrees for 10 to 12 minutes. Seeds should be lightly browned and have a toasted flavor. Cookies should be very dry. Makes 100 cookies.

Good Hope Seed Cookies

Sarah Migliore sent this seed "cake" recipe. It makes a seed biscotti very much like the ones sold by Brocato's in New Orleans.

3 lb. all-purpose flour
1½ lb. sugar
5 tbsp. baking powder
1½ lb. shortening
3 eggs
5 tsp. vanilla
1½ to 2 cups milk
⅔ cup sesame seeds

Mix all dry ingredients except seeds. Cut shortening in with fingers or a pastry blender. Beat eggs with vanilla and milk. Add liquid mixture to dry ingredients to make a soft dough. Shape dough into sausage-like rolls. Wet seeds with water and place on a damp towel. Roll dough in seeds then cut into 1-inch pieces. Bake on ungreased cookie sheet at 375 degrees for about 10 minutes or until lightly browned. Makes 120 cookies.

Kay's Seed Cookies

Kay Mortillaro submitted this recipe but wrote, "I'm not Italian. I just married one!"

3 lb. sesame seeds
5 lb. flour
5 tbsp. baking powder
2 cups shortening
3 eggs
3 cups milk
1 tsp. anise
3 tbsp. Accent or salt
4 cups sugar
3 egg whites

Wash and drain seeds the day before you bake the cookies. To prepare the cookie dough, mix flour and baking powder in the center of a clean, dry table. Blend in shortening with fingers until mixture is mealy. In a pot or bowl, combine eggs, milk, anise,

Accent, and sugar. Slowly add to flour mixture. Mix to make a soft dough that holds its shape. Knead. Let dough rest 1 hour then knead again. Cover with a clean towel. Beat 3 egg whites until fluffy then add washed seeds. Roll dough into long, skinny pieces then brush surface with seeds. Place on a greased cookie sheet and bake at 350 degrees for 15 minutes or until lightly browned and very dry. Cool before storing. Makes about 200 cookies.

Old-Fashioned Seed Biscotti

Theresa Gennusa said that her mother grew up on an olive farm near Corte Lone in Italy. The skills her mother learned while growing up on the farm helped the family when they moved to America. Theresa told me that when she was a child, her family grew most of what the family ate. They even had a goat in the back yard to provide milk for the baby of the family and to make cheese. Later, in typical Italian tradition, Theresa, who remained unmarried, took care of her parents and family. Here is one of the recipes she made for them.

1 lb. all-purpose flour
¼ cup sugar
½ cup butter or shortening
1 tsp. ammonia powder or crystals, purchased at a pharmacy
¾ cup milk
½ cup sesame seeds

In a bowl combine flour and sugar then cut in shortening with fingers or a pastry blender. Dissolve ammonia powder in milk. Add to flour mixture until dough holds together. Pull off small pieces of dough and roll into finger-like shapes. Roll in additional milk then in seeds. Cut dough in 1-inch strips. Bake on ungreased cookie sheet at 350 degrees for 20 to 25 minutes. Cool and store in airtight container. Makes 80 cookies.

Chocolate Italian Biscotti

These cookies are a little different; they are frosted with a creamy frosting. Lucille Lemendola shared this recipe with me back in the '60s. She had baked the cookies for the St. Joseph altar at the church where Fr. Robert Inzina was the pastor. He had initiated a unique custom and asked that his congregation bring canned goods to put on the altar. The pastries were shared with the visitors, and the food was given to the poor of the community.

4 cups sugar
1 lb. shortening
9 eggs
12 cups all-purpose flour
6 tsp. baking powder
2 tsp. nutmeg
1 tbsp. cloves
3 tbsp. cinnamon
3 tsp. vanilla
4 cups milk, more or less

Cream sugar, shortening, and eggs. Sift together dry ingredients. Combine vanilla and milk. Alternating with milk, add dry ingredients to sugar mixture to form a soft dough. Roll into 1-inch diameter "snakes." Cut into 2-inch strips. On 1 side of each strip, make 3 cuts with a sharp knife about ¾ of an inch apart. Bend to form a crescent. Bake on greased cookie sheet for about 15 minutes.

Icing
2 egg whites
2 tbsp. vanilla, lemon, or almond flavoring
1 lb. powdered sugar
1 tbsp. white corn syrup
Food coloring
1 tsp. cream of tartar

Beat egg whites until stiff. Add vanilla, lemon, or almond flavoring, powdered sugar, white corn syrup, a few drops of desired food coloring, and cream of tartar. Icing will be runny. Place cookies in a bowl with the frosting and toss gently as you would a salad. Spread on waxed paper or aluminum foil to dry. Makes 12 dozen cookies.

Gembrone Chocolate Spice Biscotti

(Biscotti di Cioccolato alla Gembrone)

These cookies combine chocolate and spices for an unusual taste, but they make a delicious, tasty treat. Georgette (Faucheux) Cornelius sent this recipe.

2 lb. shortening
1 lb. butter
2½ lb. sugar
12 eggs
Grated rind and juice from 2 oranges
Grated rind and juice from 2 lemons
6 lb. all-purpose flour
1 tbsp. cinnamon
1 tsp. cloves
1 cup cocoa
1 tsp. salt
7 tbsp. baking powder
1 qt. milk
2 cups walnuts or pecans, chopped

Cream shortening, butter, sugar, and eggs. Add juice and grated rind of 2 oranges and 2 lemons. Sift together flour, spices, salt, and baking powder. Add flour mixture alternately with milk. Mix well. Add nuts and mix. Knead dough until smooth then refrigerate for 2 hours. Oil hands and shape dough into small balls. Bake at 350 degrees for about 15 minutes. Makes 100 small cookies.

Chocolate-Vanilla Biscotti

Mrs. Tony Pigno of New Orleans sent another great chocolate cookie recipe. Chocolate and vanilla always go well together.

1 cup sugar
3 tbsp. shortening
2 eggs
1 tsp. vanilla
3 cups all-purpose flour
6 tsp. baking powder
1 cup cocoa
1 cup milk
½ cup pecans, chopped

Cream sugar and shortening together. Add eggs and vanilla. Sift flour with baking powder, salt, and cocoa. Add flour mixture alternately with milk to make a soft dough. Mix in pecans. Roll dough into balls about the size of a walnut. Place on greased cookie sheet and bake 10 minutes at 350 degrees. Glaze cookies with your favorite glaze. Makes 50 cookies.

Chocolate Coconut Biscotti

3 cups sugar
1½ cups shortening
2 tbsp. butter
6 eggs, beaten
3 tsp. anise flavoring
10 cups all-purpose flour
10 tsp. baking powder
¾ cup milk

Cream together sugar, shortening, and butter. Add eggs and flavoring. Beat well. Sift flour and baking powder together. Alternating with milk, add flour mixture to egg mixture. Shape into small balls. Bake at 350 degrees for 20 minutes.

Coconut glaze
1 1-lb. box powdered sugar
2 tsp. coconut flavor
¼ cup canned milk
4 cups angel flake coconut

Mix powdered sugar with coconut flavor and canned milk. Frost cookies and dip into a dish of angel flake coconut. Place on tray to dry. Makes 80 cookies.

Chocolate Rocks

Mrs. Joseph (Lombardo) Bellina always helped her sister, Mrs. Vincent Silvio, with altar cooking and baking. Often featuring these cookies, her altars were always offered in thanksgiving for recovery from illness.

2 cups sugar
1 cup butter
3 eggs
2 tsp. vanilla
8 cups flour
1 tsp. cloves
2 tsp. allspice
8 tbsp. cocoa
1 tbsp. baking powder
1 tsp. baking soda
1 cup milk
3½ cups pecans, chopped

Cream sugar and butter together until light and fluffy. Add eggs and beat well. Sift flour with spices, cocoa, baking powder, and baking soda. Combine milk and vanilla Alternating with dry ingredients, add milk to egg mixture. Stir in nuts. Shape into small balls. Bake at 350 degrees for about 10 minutes. Cookies should be very dry. Cover with glaze.

Variation
For plain rocks, omit cocoa.

Glaze
1 lb. powdered sugar
2 tbsp. butter, melted
1 tbsp. lemon juice
4 tbsp. canned milk

Make a glaze by mixing powdered sugar with melted butter, lemon juice, and canned milk. Spread over cookies. Makes 8 to 10 dozen cookies.

Independence Chocolate Rocks

In Independence, Louisiana's Little Italy, wine is used in everything from sauces to cookies. Anna Mae Fresina sent this delicious wine cookie recipe.

1 egg
1/2 cup butter or margarine
1 cup sugar
1 tbsp. shortening
3 1/4 cups flour
4 tsp. cocoa
3 tsp. allspice
1 tsp. cinnamon
1 tsp. cloves
3 1/2 tsp. baking powder
4 oz. red wine
1 cup pecans, chopped

Beat egg, butter, sugar, and shortening together until creamy. Sift together flour, cocoa, spices, and baking powder. Alternating with wine, add flour mixture to egg mixture. Add pecans. Oil hands and shape dough into small balls. Bake at 350 degrees for 10 minutes. Makes 8 to 10 dozen cookies.

Cocoons

Bonnie Richie Tregre, who hails from North Claiborne Avenue in New Orleans, said, "Don't forget the cocoons." Cocoons are the American version of the *Fave dei Morti*, or Beans of the Dead, and are eaten on November 2, All Soul's Day (*Il Giorno dei Morti*). This is not a gloomy day in Italy. On this day engagements are announced and rings are given to sweethearts. Traditionally, a young man would send a ring to his fiancée in a small oval box filled with the Fave dei Morti.

1 cup butter
3 tbsp. granulated sugar
2 cups all-purpose flour
1 tsp. vanilla
1 cup pecans or almonds, finely chopped
1 cup powdered sugar

Cream butter and granulated sugar together. Mix in flour, vanilla, and nuts. Shape into small "cocoons." Place on ungreased cookie sheet and bake at 350 degrees for 15 to 20 minutes. While cookies are still hot, roll them in powdered sugar. Makes 24 cookies.

Fave dei Morti

This is the "real" recipe for the Beans of the Dead. It was shared by Georgette (Faucheux) Cornelius.

½ cup butter
⅔ cup sugar
2 eggs
2 cups all-purpose flour
1 tsp. vanilla or grated lemon rind
1 cup pistachio nuts, finely ground

Cream butter and sugar together. Add eggs one at a time, beating well after each addition. Stir in remaining ingredients. Refrigerate dough for 1 hour. Form dough into small, kidney-shaped "beans." Place on greased cookie sheet and bake at 350 degrees for 10 to 12 minutes. Makes 24 cookies.

Scadelina

These cookies are also known as *Orso di Mortis*, or Bones of the Dead. Mrs. Jack Pizzalota gave me this recipe, for which I had been searching for years.

½ cup water
1½ cups sugar
½ tsp. cinnamon
3 cups flour

Bring water, sugar, and cinnamon to a boil. Add flour, stir, and remove from heat. Roll dough into finger-sized lengths and cut into 2-inch pieces. Place on cookie sheets or parchment paper to dry for 2 days. Bake at 400 degrees for about 20 minutes or until cookies are dry and hard. Makes 2 dozen cookies.

Dead Man Bones

These cookies are very much like the kind you can buy at Brocato's in New Orleans. I can't divulge the source of this recipe, but my mother made theses cookies for my first St. Joseph altar.

2 cups granulated sugar
1 cup all-purpose flour
1/8 tsp. baking powder
1 tsp. cinnamon
1/8 tsp. cloves
3/4 tsp. allspice
1/4 cup water

Mix all ingredients with water to make stiff dough. Shape dough into long snakelike forms. Cut into 2-inch pieces and place on cookie sheets or parchment paper to dry overnight. Bake at 350 degrees for about 15 minutes. Makes 20 pieces.

Cuccidati

(*Buccelato*)

These intricately designed fig cakes are found on all St. Joseph altars. Here in Louisiana both the small and large fig cakes are called cuccidati, but technically the large cakes are buccelato. This pastry is made into many different shapes. Among them are the monstrance, chalice, wreath, heart of Jesus, palm, St. Joseph sandal, and rooster.

4 cups milk
1 1/2 cups shortening
1/4 tsp. salt
1 cup sugar
1 1/2 tsp. vanilla
1 1/2 tsp. anise extract
3 eggs
8 cups all-purpose flour
3 tbsp. baking powder

Warm milk. Add shortening, salt, sugar, and vanilla and anise extracts. Beat eggs. Add milk mixture to eggs and beat until fluffy and light. Sift flour and baking powder together. Add to milk and eggs. Mix well. Knead dough lightly. Let rest 15 minutes. Roll dough out and cut into desired shapes. Make decorative cutouts with an aspic cutter or use a paring knife to cut shapes. Cut out 2 of each shape. Cover the surface of 1 of each shape with a layer of filling.

Filling
1/2 lb. dried figs
1/2 lb. raisins
1 orange
1/4 lb. citron
1/4 cup honey
1/4 tsp. cinnamon
1/4 tsp. black pepper
1/4 tsp. allspice
1 cup pecans

Grind figs, raisins, orange, and citron. Add honey, spices, and nuts. Spread filling over surface of dough shapes. Place long skewers under filling to provide support. Place corresponding shape over the filling and use a fork or imprint a decorative design to seal edges. Bake at 325 degrees for 25 minutes or until lightly browned. Makes 6 large decorative cakes.

These are edible decorative pieces. Additional support can be given to these cakes by mounting them on aluminum-covered cardboard cutouts using a powdered-sugar frosting.

Small Cuccidati

To make small cakes, roll dough into pieces about 3 inches wide. Place filling on one side of the dough. Lap over and seal edge with a little water. Cut into 2-inch lengths. Bake at 375 degrees for 12 minutes or until lightly browned. Makes 8 dozen cookies.

Note: All small fig cookies may be shaped using directions on page 156.

Fig "Cakes"

Claire Poretto of Houma sent this cuccidati recipe, a family favorite.

16 cups all-purpose flour
1½ tsp. salt
4 cups shortening or butter
3 cups sugar
4 cups warm water, more or less

Sift flour and salt together. Cut shortening into flour using a pastry blender. Dissolve sugar in warm water and add to flour. Mix well. Let dough rest for 1 hour. Roll dough to ⅛-inch thickness. Cut into 3-inch strips. Cover with a damp cloth and prepare filling.

Filling
1 fresh orange
5 lb. dried figs
2 15-oz. boxes raisins
2 cups pecans
2 tbsp. pure vanilla
2 tsp. cinnamon
1 tsp. allspice
1½ cups sugar
1 cup warm water

Cut orange into 8 pieces. Finely chop orange, figs, raisins, and pecans in a food processor. Add vanilla and spices. Mix sugar with warm water and add to mixture. Mix thoroughly. Place a layer of filling on dough. Lap over and seal edges with a little water. Cut into 1-inch pieces. Bake at 350 degrees for 15 minutes or until lightly browned. Makes 16 dozen cookies.

Fig Pastry

Mrs. Albert Culmone says that she has special tools to use for decorating her fig pastry. Her odds-and-ends collection includes a curved piece of an old metal hair roller. These tools are kept in a special box and are brought out only to be used for decorating her very special and beautiful fig pastries. The filling for this cake is flavored with black pepper as well as "sweet spices."

12 cups all-purpose flour
1½ cups sugar
5½ tsp. baking powder
½ tsp. salt
1 cup butter
1 cup shortening
6 eggs
1¾ cups milk, more or less
3 tbsp. vanilla

Sift dry ingredients together. Blend in butter and shortening with a pastry blender as you would to make pie dough. Beat eggs, milk, and vanilla together. Add to dry ingredients and mix well. Roll out dough and cut into desired shapes. With filling, cover cutout to ½ inch from the edge. Cover with another layer of dough and trim to shape of bottom layer of dough. Seal edges. Using a paring knife or aspic cutter, decorate as desired. Makes 6 decorative, edible pastries.

Filling
2 lb. dried figs
1 orange
1 cup fig preserves
1 tbsp. allspice
1 tbsp. black pepper
1 tbsp. vanilla

Wash dried figs. Grind figs, orange, and preserves in a food processor. Add remaining ingredients. Mix well.

Mrs. Mortillaro's Fig Cookies

Kay Mortillaro says that it is hard to find a bowl big enough to mix this recipe so she mixes the cookie dough on her table.

5 lb. all-purpose flour
5 tbsp. baking powder
2 cups shortening
3 cups sugar
4 tbsp. anise flavoring
3 tbsp. Accent or salt
3 cups milk
3 eggs
Broomstick cut into 8-inch length, unpainted

Mix flour and baking powder in the center of the table. Work shortening in with fingers like you would for pie dough. Sift dry ingredients together. Mix milk and eggs in a bowl then slowly add to dry ingredients. Mix with hands until dough is smooth. You might need a little extra liquid. Let dough rest for about 1 hour. Knead lightly then cover with a towel. Scrub and dry broomstick. Use broomstick to roll dough to 1/8-inch thickness. Cut into 3-inch strips. Prepare filling.

Filling
1 large orange
1 large lemon
1 16-oz. can fruit cocktail
5 lb. dried figs
1 lb. dates
4 cups sugar
2 cups pecans, finely chopped

Peel orange and lemon. Place in a 325-degree oven and bake until very dry. Place dried fruit in a blender to pulverize or mash with a hammer to make into a powder. Put fruit powder as well as juices and fruit of fruit cocktail in a blender to puree. Grind figs and dates. Place all ingredients in a bowl and mix well with your hands. Place filling on dough. Pinch sides of dough together and seal edges with a little water. Cut into 1 1/2-inch pieces and place on a greased cookie sheet. Bake at 350 degrees for about 15 minutes. Frost with your favorite powdered-sugar glaze if desired. Makes 25 dozen cookies

500 Fig Cookies

Mrs. Joe Vullo of New Orleans promised an altar to St. Joseph over 60 years ago when she and her husband were very ill. For her altar, she made her fig cakes in the shapes of cones, palms, baskets, crosses, fish, and Mary's bleeding heart.

40 lb. all-purpose flour
10 lb. sugar
4 tbsp. salt
16 lb. shortening
8 oz. vanilla flavor
2 gal. water, more or less

Mix flour, sugar, and salt together. Cut shortening in with fingers or use a commercial mixer. Add vanilla and enough water to make a stiff dough.

Filling
20 lb. dried figs
1 cup grated orange peel
3 cups pecans, finely chopped
4 tbsp. cinnamon
10 1-lb. boxes raisins
2 16-oz. bottles corn syrup

Grind solid ingredients together. Add syrup to soften mixture. Place this mixture in a large pot and cook until it is firm. Cool. Place filling on dough. Pinch sides of dough together and seal edges with a little water. Cut into 1½-inch pieces and place on a greased cookie sheet. Bake at 350 degrees for about 15 minutes. Frost with your favorite powdered-sugar glaze if desired. Makes 500 cookies.

Shirley's Fig Cookies

This is a fig cookie recipe from my friend Shirley Vicknair. Shirley is known on the West Bank of New Orleans for both her culinary and sewing skills. She was an innovator in Mardi Gras costume design and construction and just recently retired.

5 lb. all-purpose flour
2 tsp. nutmeg
2 tsp. cinnamon
10 tsp. baking powder
2 cups sugar
2½ cups shortening
2 cups butter
1 13-oz. can milk
8 eggs
1 cup whole milk
4 oz. almond flavoring

Sift all dry ingredients together. Blend in shortening with a pastry blender. Beat liquid ingredients together. Add to dry mixture and mix well. Prepare Claire Poretto's Fig "Cakes" filling (p. 154); it is very much like Shirley's with the wonderful flavor of orange rind. Makes 20 dozen cookies.

Fig Preserves

If the Italians immigrating to Louisiana found their new environment forbidding, perhaps the ability to grow familiar fruits in this land eased their adjustment to an area fraught with new challenges.

2½ qt. fresh figs, rinsed well
5 cups sugar
¼ cup water

Place all ingredients in a heavy 5-quart pot. Bring to a boil. Reduce heat and cook about 1½ hours until the figs have turned brown and syrup is of desired consistency. Place in sterilized jars. Clean top of jar with a clean, damp cloth. Seal with a new rubberized lid and screw top. Process in hot water bath for 10 minutes. Remove jars from water and let cool to room temperature. Preserves will keep indefinitely. Makes 2 quarts of preserves.

Fig Preserve Layer Cake

The Italian immigrants must have rejoiced to find fig trees growing in their new homeland for fig trees, as well as citrus orchards, were part of the farming landscape in the old country.

2 cups flour
1 tsp. cinnamon
1 tsp. nutmeg
½ tsp. ground cloves
1 tsp. baking soda
1 tsp. salt
1½ cups sugar
1 tsp. vanilla
1 cup oil
2 eggs
1 cup buttermilk
1 cup fig preserves
1 cup pecans, chopped

Sift all dry ingredients together. Mix together vanilla, oil, eggs, and buttermilk. In a bowl combine dry ingredients with liquid mixture. Beat well. Remove stems from figs. Chop figs then stir into batter. Add pecans. Mix well. Grease and flour 2 8-inch by 8-inch cake pans. Spread batter into pans and bake at 325 degrees for approximately 30 minutes. Cool and frost with cream cheese frosting.

Cream Cheese Frosting
1 9-oz. package cream cheese
½ cup Crisco shortening
½ cup butter or margarine
1 tsp. vanilla
1 tsp. almond
1 lb. box powdered sugar
Pecan halves (optional)

Beat cream cheese, Crisco, and butter until smooth. Add remaining ingredients and mix well. Frost each layer of cake. Stack layers and garnish with pecan halves if desired. Makes 8 servings.

Fruit Cookies

Annie (Joe) Zito gave me this recipe, which she always made for weddings, Christmas, and St. Joseph's Day.

8 eggs
2 cups butter or shortening
2 cups sugar
9 cups all-purpose flour
9 tsp. baking powder
1 No. 202 can crushed pineapple
3 cups pecans, chopped
1 lb. candied fruit, chopped

Cream together eggs, butter, and sugar until fluffy. Sift flour and baking powder together and add to egg mixture. Add pineapple with juice and remaining ingredients. Stir well. Drop by spoonfuls onto a greased cookie sheet. Bake at 350 degrees until lightly browned. Cookies will be soft.

Glaze
1 can condensed milk
1 lb. powdered sugar
2 tsp. grated orange rind

Mix condensed milk with powdered sugar and grated orange rind. Dip cool cookies into glaze and place on waxed paper or aluminum to dry. Makes 100 cookies.

Toronne

Many variations of this candy can be made by changing nuts and flavorings.

2½ cups plus 2 tbsp. sugar
¾ cup plus 1 tbsp. light corn syrup
½ cup plus 1 tbsp. water
⅛ tsp. salt
⅓ cup egg whites
1½ tsp. vanilla
½ tsp. almond flavoring
1 cup unblanched almonds, coarsely chopped

Butter an 8-inch by 8-inch pan and set aside. Combine sugar, corn syrup, and water in a 2-quart pot with a heavy bottom. Stir and cook over medium heat until syrup mixture reaches 270 degrees, the soft-crack stage. While syrup is cooking, add salt to egg whites and beat to a soft peak with an electric mixer. When syrup reaches the soft-crack stage, pour over egg whites in a steady stream while continuously beating the mixture. Stir in flavoring and nuts. Continue beating another 10 minutes by hand. Pour mixture into the buttered pan and spread. Let set over night before cutting. Makes 16 pieces.

Geegees

When Gail Bosco says "geegees," her eyes light up. Apparently a family favorite, this must be the Italian "popcorn" that I've heard so much about!

9 eggs
5 cups all-purpose flour
Oil for frying
1 lb. powdered sugar
1/4 cup canned milk, more or less

Beat eggs until light. Add flour gradually and mix in thoroughly. Shape dough into long, thin "snakes." Cut into marble-sized pieces and fry at 370 degrees until golden brown. Drain and cool. Mix powdered sugar with about 1/4 cup canned milk to make a glaze. Put geegees into bowl with glaze and mix so that each is covered. Separate and place on cookie sheet to dry. Makes about 3 quarts of small pieces.

Honey Clusters

(*Strufoli*)

My Uncle Edgar Faucheux's mouth watered as he described the bags of goodies he received from Italian friends each year. One of his favorite sweets was strufoli, another version of Italian "popcorn."

3 cups all-purpose flour
3 eggs
2 cups salad oil

Place flour into a bowl. Make a well in the center and add eggs. Mix well. Knead dough until smooth and no longer sticky. Shape into marble-sized balls. Fry in hot oil until brown.

Glaze
1½ cups honey
½ cup sugar

Combine honey and sugar in a heavy pot. Cook on medium heat until contents reach the hard-crack stage, between 300 and 310 degrees. Drizzle over strufoli and shape pieces into clusters while still hot. Makes 24 small clusters.

Hint
Use a candy thermometer to gauge temperature or drop a teaspoon of syrup into a cup of cold water. If mixture hardens immediately, it has reached the hard-crack stage.

Dat Italian Praline Cookie

Vicki DiMaggio Woodall shared this recipe for baked pralines, which are always a hit. I don't know of anyone who has eaten one of these pralines and did not think they were delicious.

¼ tsp. salt
2 egg whites
1 tsp. vanilla
1 cup brown sugar
5 cups pecan halves

Add salt to egg whites and beat until frothy then add vanilla. Add sugar to the eggs a little at a time. Beat to form a stiff meringue. Add pecans. Drop dough by spoonfuls onto well-buttered foil and place on a cookie sheet. Bake at 300 degrees for 30 minutes or until firm and dry. Turn oven off and let cookies remain in oven for 45 minutes. Makes 2 dozen cookies.

Florentines

This delightful little biscuit from Florence is famous around the world. They can be made in a smaller size to serve with your after-dinner coffee.

1/4 cup almonds
1/4 cup walnuts
1 tbsp. raisins
1 tbsp. mixed peel
5 candied cherries
3 pieces candied ginger
2 oz. butter
1/4 cup sugar
1 tbsp. cream
4 oz. dark chocolate, chopped

Finely chop almonds and walnuts. Mix raisins, peel, cherries, and ginger. Add fruit to nut mixture. Melt butter in small saucepan. Add sugar and stir over gentle heat until sugar dissolves. Bring to a boil. Boil gently for 1 minute. Do not stir while boiling or mixture will crystallize. When mixture begins to turn a light golden color, remove from heat. Add butter mixture and cream to fruit and nut mixture. Mix well. Spoon heaping teaspoonfuls of mixture onto greased oven trays, allowing room between each for spreading. Four Florentines will fit on 1 tray. Bake in a 325-degree oven for 10 minutes or until golden brown. Remove from tray with spatula. Push each Florentine into round shape. Allow to cool on trays 1 minute. Then, with spatula carefully lift each Florentine from tray onto wire cooling rack. Allow to cool and become firm.

Place chopped chocolate in top of double saucepan. Stir over simmering water until chocolate has melted. Allow chocolate to cool slightly. Turn Florentines over so that the flat side is facing up. Spoon 1 teaspoon of chocolate onto flat side and spread to edge of biscuit. When chocolate is almost set, run a fork through the chocolate to create a wave-like effect. Place on tray and refrigerate until chocolate has set. Store in airtight container. Makes 3 dozen cookies.

Clove Cake

(Panedi Chiodo di Garofano)

Matilda Matteo's daughter, Patty Amato, sent the recipe for this unusual cake. In Italian, the cake is called *Panedi Chiodo di Garofano*. Who can pronounce that? She probably had help with the pronunciation from her many Italian relatives, among them Gloria and Charles Tadaro, Connie Sierra, and Virginia Gennusa.

2 cups butter
4 cups sugar
8 eggs
1 tbsp. cloves
2 tsp. baking powder
2 tbsp. nutmeg
2 tbsp. cloves
2 tbsp. cinnamon
8 oz. whiskey
2 boxes raisins
4 cups pecans, chopped
½ cup maraschino cherries, drained
8 oz. candied citron
Flour
2 tsp. baking powder

Cream butter and sugar together until light and lemon colored. Add eggs 1 at a time, beating well after each addition. Sift dry ingredients together. Alternating with whiskey, add the dry ingredient mixture a little at a time to the egg mixture. Dredge raisins, nuts, cherries, and citron in flour. Stir raisins, cherries, nuts, and citron into mixture. Bake at 350 degrees in 2 greased and floured Bundt pans for 1 hour or until top springs back when lightly touched. Makes 20 servings.

Pinulatas

When Sister Martin Culotta retired after nearly 50 years of teaching, she decided that she wanted to make an altar for the "old" people in the retirement home where she was living. She called me to make pinulatas, which are always found on St. Joseph altars. Though Sister Culotta had many Italian nieces, I, the French-German wife of her Italian nephew, was asked to make Italian pastries for her altar. I was so honored. Consequently, my mother and I spent many hours together learning to make pinulatas. I treasure the memories.

This is Ruth Lussan Horn's recipe. Paul Kleinpeter of Donaldsonville, Louisiana, also sent a similar recipe for pinulatas.

6 tbsp. butter
6 cups all-purpose flour
12 eggs
Oil for frying
6 cups sugar
½ cup honey

Using your fingers, work butter into flour. Beat eggs until light and pour into flour. Mix well. Knead dough on a lightly floured surface. Shape into pencil-sized "snakes." With a sharp knife cut dough at an angle into ¼-inch pieces. Fry in hot oil until browned then drain. Melt sugar in a heavy pot. Add honey and cook to hard-crack stage, between 300 and 310 degrees on a candy thermometer. Sugar will get lumpy but continue to cook until it is brown and turns to a smooth liquid. Pour syrup over the fried dough pieces and, using an oiled funnel, form into "pine cone" shaped mounds. Be careful; the syrup is very hot and could cause serious burns. Makes 4 large "cones."

Hint

If the sugar has reached the hard-crack stage, when a bit of syrup is dropped into a cup of cold water, the liquid will harden immediately.

"Shrimp" Cookies

Anna Mae Fresina of Independence visited with relatives in Italy nearly 30 years ago. Upon her return she sent me this cookie recipe with its deceptive title. I suspect the color of this cookie gives it its "fishy" name.

¼ tsp. salt
4 cups all-purpose flour
10 tbsp. powdered sugar
2 cups pecans, chopped
¾ cup butter, melted

Blend dry ingredients together then add nuts and melted butter. Mix well. Chill for 1 hour. After dough has chilled, form small pieces of dough into a crescent shrimp-like shape. Bake at 325 degrees for 12 to 15 minutes.

Glaze
2 drops red food coloring
2 drops yellow food coloring
1 lb. powdered sugar
4 tbsp. canned milk

Combine all ingredients. Dip cookies in glaze and place on a cookie sheet to dry. Makes 40 cookies.

Rosary Cake

Mr. and Mrs. Conrad Klein of New Orleans were known for their beautiful rosary cakes, baked especially for the St. Joseph altar by their friends, Mr. and Mrs. E. O. Link. Each rosary cake was unique and every cookie "bead" was decorated differently. One year, in keeping with the popularity of the "guitar mass," the cake was arranged in the shape of a guitar.

Pink Cookie Rosary

Gail Bosco made this cookie rosary for my first St. Joseph altar. This combination of cherry and vanilla makes for a very flavorful cookie.

7 eggs
2¼ cups sugar
1 tbsp. vanilla
1½ cups melted butter
1 8-oz. jar maraschino cherries, drained and chopped; reserve juice
1 cup pecan, chopped
7 cups flour
7 tsp. baking powder

Beat eggs, sugar, and vanilla until light and fluffy. Beat in melted butter. Add chopped cherries, half of cherry juice, and nuts. Sift flour and baking powder together and add to egg mixture. Roll dough into balls to make "beads" of rosary. Shape one piece of dough for the cross. Place on greased cookie sheet and bake at 375 degrees for 9 minutes. Cool.

Glaze
Reserved cherry juice
1 lb. powdered sugar
2 tbsp. canned milk or enough to make a soft glaze

Mix remaining cherry juice with powdered sugar and canned milk to make a glaze. Dip in glaze and place in the shape of a rosary on waxed paper or foil to dry. Makes enough cookies for 1 rosary.

Taralli

Mary (Liberto) Cascio was born in Sicily to Dorothy and Phillip Liberto on July 14, 1898. Her father came to the United States in 1900, docking in New Orleans. From there he went to Shreveport, where he worked at the St. Vincent School to save money so that he could bring his family to America. Mary soon came to Louisiana, where she married Vincent Mafassa when she was 15 years old. At the age of 20, she was a widow with 3 children. She married Anthony Cascio, who had 5 children. Together they had 5 children, making a grand total of 13 children, 6 boys and 7 girls—a large Italian family. Coming from a family that represents the path of many Italian immigrants to Louisiana, who better than Mary to provide this traditional recipe for taralli?

2 cups sugar
1/4 cup butter
6 eggs
2 tbsp. vanilla
1/8 tsp. salt
4 cups all-purpose flour
1 tsp. baking powder

Cream sugar and butter together. Beat in eggs and vanilla. Sift together salt, flour, and baking powder. Add to egg mixture and beat well. Drop by tablespoons onto a greased cookie sheet. Bake at 350 degrees for approximately 15 minutes. Makes 50 cookies.

Turk's Head

(*Tasa de Turka*)

Perhaps the colorful turbans worn by the Turks years ago inspired Tasa de Turka. This is a special pastry made by Delia and Annie Cashio of Baton Rouge, who drizzle the "tasa" with red and yellow powdered-sugar glazes.

2 eggs
1/4 cup milk
2 cups flour
3 qt. oil

Beat eggs and milk together. Add flour and mix well. Knead on board until dough is firm. Let rest 15 minutes. Knead dough again. Stretch dough as you would for making a pizza but form it into a rectangular shape. Cut dough in half with a clean, sharp knife. Beginning 1 inch from the end of the dough, cut 3 parallel slices the length of the dough. You should have created several strips of dough still attached to each other at both ends. Heat oil in a deep fryer or deep, heavy pot to 370 degrees. Gather the uncut edges of the dough like pleats and pinch dough together. Place the tines of a fork in each gathered end. Gently lift the dough and gradually drop into hot oil until pastry is completely covered with oil. As pastry is placed in the oil, the strips of dough will rise and spread out. Cook until the pastry is light brown. Drain.

Glaze
2 cups powdered sugar
½ tsp. red food coloring
3 tbsp. water
½ tsp. yellow food coloring

Mix 1 cup powdered sugar with red food coloring and 1½ tablespoons water. Repeat process with yellow food coloring. Drizzle colored glazes over pastry. Makes 2 pastries.

Ice Box Cookies

Mrs. Joe Marino of Baton Rouge makes this cookie for special family occasions.

2 cups white sugar
1 cup brown sugar
2 cups butter or margarine
4 eggs
8 cups all-purpose flour
1 tsp. baking powder
1 cup pecans, chopped
1½ tbsp. vanilla

Cream sugar and butter together. Add eggs and beat well. Sift flour and baking powder together and add to sugar mixture. Add nuts and vanilla. Roll dough into a loaf about the diameter of a broomstick. Wrap in foil and refrigerate overnight. When ready to bake, cut dough into slices and place on an ungreased cookie sheet. Bake at 375 degrees for about 10 minutes. Makes 48 cookies.

Ricotta Cream Cannoli

Monsignor Salvatore Culotta said that on a recent trip to Italy he was told that "cannolo" is singular and "cannoli" is plural. Whether or not they are referred to by the proper form, these pastries are always delightful. Here is a cannoli recipe from Theresa Gennussa, who was in her 80s when I first interviewed her. I hope she is smiling down from heaven at me now that this book is being published.

Cannoli shells
4 cups all-purpose flour
1 tbsp. sugar
1/4 tsp. sugar
1/4 tsp. cinnamon
3/4 cup dry red wine
6-inch lengths of 1-inch dowel rods or cannoli molds
1 egg yolk, slightly beaten
Oil for frying

Sift flour, sugar, and cinnamon together on a breadboard. Make a well in the center of the dry ingredients. Pour wine into the well. Mix by hand to make a smooth dough. Knead well. If dough is too moist, add more flour; if dough is too dry, add more wine. Cover with a damp cloth and let rest for 2 hours in a cool place. Roll to paper thickness. Cut into 5-inch rounds. Form around rods or molds, overlapping ends and sealing with a little egg yolk. Fry in hot oil until crisp. Drain and cool. Fill with ricotta filling. Unfilled shells will keep for about 6 weeks in an airtight container.

Cannoli Filling
3 lb. ricotta
1 3/4 cups powdered sugar
1/2 tsp. cinnamon
2 tbsp. chopped citron
1/4 cup semi-sweet chocolate morsels, chopped

Drain ricotta and place in a large bowl. Add powdered sugar, cinnamon, and citron. Using a pastry tube, stuff each shell with filling. Garnish ends of cannoli with chocolate bits or chopped pistachios. Makes 24 cannoli.

Pastry Cream Cannoli

As a child, my mother-in-law, Angelina Josephina Culotta Wilson, spent time in Chicago. One day a young man asked, "What are you, anyway? Jewish?" She replied, "Can't you see the map of Italy on my face?" The family joke is that you can tell an Italian either by his name or his nose.

My mother-in-law said that her Aunt Liva used to make cannoli, and her sister-in-law, Aunt Lena, said that true Italian cannoli requires preserved watermelon rind in the ricotta cream. Here, however, is a non-ricotta version of this Italian favorite.

Cannoli shells
3 cups cake flour
¼ cup sugar
3 tbsp. shortening
¼ cup water
¼ cup white wine

Combine flour and sugar. Cut shortening into flour with a pastry blender. Add liquids and mix well. Knead until smooth then divide dough into walnut-sized pieces. Roll into rounds. Form dough around dowel rods or cannoli shell molds. Seal overlapping edges with a little water.

Custard filling
2 cups milk
4 cinnamon sticks
1½ cups sugar
4 tbsp. cornstarch
1 jigger white wine
½ jigger vanilla

Scald 1 cup milk. Add cinnamon sticks. When milk is cool, remove cinnamon sticks and add sugar. Mix cornstarch with remaining milk. Cook over low heat until mixture begins to boil. Continue cooking at a boil for 3 minutes. Stir in wine and vanilla. Cool. Fill shells. Makes 8 cannoli.

Sicilian Cheesecake

Cookie Crust
¾ cup plain chocolate cookies
⅓ cup butter

Filling
1¼ lb. Ricotta cheese
1 cup powdered sugar
1 tsp. vanilla
2 tbsp. crème de cacao
2 oz. dark chocolate
2 tbsp. dried fruit, chopped
2 oz. dark chocolate, extra
½ cup cream

Finely crush chocolate cookies and add melted butter. Press evenly over bottom of a spring-form pan. Refrigerate while preparing filling. In a mixing bowl, combine cheese, sugar, vanilla, and crème de cacao. Beat until smooth and fluffy. Grate chocolate finely. Add dried fruit and chocolate to cheese mixture; mix thoroughly. Spoon filling over crumb crust. Refrigerate overnight or at least 6 hours. Before serving, whip cream until soft peaks form then spread evenly over top of cake. Grate extra chocolate and sprinkle around edges. Makes 8 servings.

Italian Cream Cake

This is a short-cut version of the original. Though not quite as good as the real thing, it is a great fake, and I have fooled my family for years with this cake.

1 box white cake mix
1 tsp. vanilla
1 tsp. almond flavoring
10 oz. angel flake coconut
1 cup toasted pecans or almonds, finely chopped

Place cake mix, flavorings, coconut, and nuts in bowl. Prepare mix according to package instructions. Bake in 2 greased and floured 8-inch square pans according to instructions. Cool and split cakes to make 4 layers.

Frosting
1 cup butter or margarine
1/2 cup shortening
8 oz. cream cheese
1 tsp. vanilla
2 tsp. almond flavoring

Beat together butter or margarine, shortening, cream cheese, and vanilla and almond flavorings until light and fluffy. Frost each cake layer and stack to make a 4-layer cake. Garnish with additional toasted, chopped nuts. Makes 8 to 10 servings.

Lamb Cake

Nina Sharp sent this recipe for her lamb cakes. A good pound-cake mix can be used for ease in preparation. You will also need lamb-cake pans. Theresa Gennussa also made lamb cakes and put red bows on the necks of her lambs. A very talented lady, she loved to cook, bake, and crochet. She told me about crocheting edging on feed sacks, which were used for diapers for her sister's children, and crocheting her sister's wedding dress, as well as christening dresses.

2 cups all-purpose flour
2 1/2 tsp. baking powder
3/4 tsp. salt
1 cup sugar
1/2 cup shortening
3/4 cup milk
1 tsp. vanilla
3 egg whites
1 cup angel flake coconut
2 raisins
1 candied cherry

Sift all dry ingredients together. Cut shortening in with a pastry blender or with your fingers. Add milk and vanilla. Mix well then beat with an electric mixer. Beat egg whites until stiff then fold into mixture. Grease and flour 2 lamb-cake pans. Pour batter into each pan. Bake at 350 degrees for about 25 minutes. Remove from oven and cool. Frost each cake layer. Stack cake layers and frost with your favorite white frosting. Sprinkle with coconut. Use raisins for eyes and a piece of cherry for mouth. Bells are sometimes placed on a red ribbon around the lamb's neck. Makes 8 to 10 servings.

Hershey Bar Cake

This very rich pound cake is great when served with vanilla ice cream.

1 cup butter
2 cups sugar
1 tsp. vanilla
1/8 tsp. salt
8 plain chocolate Hershey bars, melted
2 1/2 cups all-purpose flour, sifted
1/4 tsp. baking soda
1 cup pecans, chopped

Cream butter and sugar. Add vanilla and salt then beat in melted chocolate. Add flour and baking soda and mix well. Stir in pecans. Place in a greased and floured Bundt-cake pan and bake at 300 degrees for about 90 minutes. Makes 12 servings.

Banana Pound Cake

This is great as a dessert or breakfast bread.

1 1/2 cups butter or margarine
2 cups sugar
4 eggs
2 cups mashed bananas
1/4 cup milk
2 tbsp. lemon juice
1 tsp. vanilla
3 cups all-purpose flour
1 1/4 tsp. baking soda
1/4 tsp. salt
1/2 cup pecans, coarsely chopped

Combine butter and sugar. Add eggs and beat well. Add bananas, milk, lemon juice, vanilla, flour, baking soda, and salt. Using an electric mixer, beat on low until all ingredients are well blended. Stir in pecans. Pour batter into a greased and floured tube pan. Bake at 325 degrees for 30 minutes or until a wooden toothpick inserted in cake comes out clean. Cool and remove from pan. Makes 10 servings.

Orange Cake

Among Italian immigrants oranges were served not only as a refreshing beverage but also were made into wine and used to flavor cookies and cakes.

1 cup butter
2 cups sugar
4 eggs
1½ cups buttermilk
4 cups all-purpose flour
2 tsp. baking soda
½ tsp. salt
1 tbsp. grated orange rind
8 oz. dates, chopped
1 cup pecans, chopped
1 cup orange juice concentrate
1 cup sugar

Cream butter and sugar and stir in orange rind. When mixture is light and fluffy, add eggs 1 at a time, beating well after each addition. Sift together flour, soda, and salt. Add to egg mixture, alternating with buttermilk until all is incorporated into the batter. Stir in dates and pecans. Place in a greased and floured tube pan or Bundt-cake pan and bake at 350 degrees for about 45 minutes. Poke holes in the cake using a fork. Mix orange juice concentrate and sugar and pour over cake. Makes 12 servings.

Lemon Gelato

½ cup sugar
½ cup water
½ cup sweet or dry wine
½ cup lemon juice
1 egg white

Place sugar, water, and wine in small pan. Stir over low heat until sugar is dissolved. Bring to boil, reduce heat, and simmer uncovered for 10 minutes. Stir strained lemon juice into cooled mixture and mix well. Pour mixture into shallow tin and freeze approximately 1 hour or until mixture is slightly firm. Remove from freezer. Turn mixture into bowl then beat with fork until smooth. Fold in firmly beaten egg white, return to tin, and freeze until firm. Makes 2 servings.

Wine and Cinnamon Cookies

My husband, the winemaker in the family, also loves this cookie recipe.

1/2 cup soft butter
1 1/3 cup brown sugar
1 egg
1 tsp. pure almond flavoring
1/2 cup almonds, finely chopped
3 cups all-purpose flour
1/2 tsp. baking powder
3/4 tsp. cinnamon
2 to 3 tbsp. red wine

Cream butter, brown sugar, and egg until mixture is light. Add remaining ingredients and mix well. On a floured surface, roll dough into half-inch snakelike shapes. Cut in 2-inch pieces. Using a paring knife, make 2 cuts half way into the side of the "snake." Curve the cookie to make a crescent. Bake at 400 degrees for about 12 minutes. This is a hard, dry cookie great with coffee or wine. Makes 3 dozen cookies.

Italian Wine Cookies

This is my husband's favorite cookie. Use leftover dinner wine or your favorite sherry.

1 cup butter
2 cups sugar
2 egg yolks
5 cups sifted all-purpose flour
1/8 tsp. salt
2/3 cup wine
1 cup pecans, chopped

Cream together butter and sugar. Add egg yolks and beat well. Combine remaining ingredients. Mix well. Knead. Chill dough 1 hour then shape into balls or small oblongs. Bake at 350 degrees for 10 minutes or until cookies are crisp. No frosting necessary. Makes 50 cookies.

Pizzelles

You will need an electric pizzelle baker to make these cookies. My husband surprised me with an antique pizzelle baker that he found while shopping in Hattiesburg, Mississippi, for a wooden canteen.

3 eggs
10 tbsp. margarine, melted
2 tsp. vanilla, anise, or almond flavoring
3/4 cup sugar
2 cups flour
2 tsp. baking powder

Using an electric mixer, beat eggs. Add margarine, flavoring, and sugar and beat mixture until smooth. Sift flour and baking powder into mixture and mix well. Dough will be sticky. Drop dough by teaspoonfuls onto the center of the bottom of each plate of the pizzelle baker. Bake pizzelles for 30 seconds or until they are golden brown. Serve as cookies or with ice cream to make ice cream sandwiches. Makes 30 pizzelles.

Toffee Bars

St. Joseph must have had a sweet tooth because nary a St. Joseph altar exists without a vast selection of candy, cookies, and fudge.

1 cup oil
1/4 cup granulated sugar
1/4 cup brown sugar
1 egg
1/4 tsp. salt
1 tsp. vanilla
1/2 cup flour
1/2 cup rolled oats
1 cup semi-sweet chocolate pieces
1/2 cup chopped pecans

In a large bowl combine oil, sugars, egg, salt, vanilla, flour, and rolled oats. Spread in a greased 9-inch square pan. Bake at 350 degrees for 20 to 25 minutes. Remove from oven and sprinkle chocolate pieces over baked cookie. As chocolate melts, spread with a knife. Sprinkle nuts over chocolate. Cool and cut into squares. Makes 9 squares.

Pecan Lace

These delicate cookies are easy to make, but you can only work with a few at a time.

1/2 cup pecans, finely chopped
2/3 cup butter
1 cup brown sugar
1/4 cup light corn syrup
1 tbsp. milk
1/4 tsp. salt
1 1/2 cups old-fashioned rolled oats (not instant oats)
2 tbsp. all-purpose flour
2 tsp. vanilla

Line 3 cookie sheets with aluminum foil. Grease well. Spread pecans over aluminum foil and toast in a 350-degree oven for about 6 minutes. Watch pecans carefully as they can burn very quickly. Set aside. Raise temperature of oven to 375 degrees. Heat butter in a small pan until it just begins to boil. Add brown sugar, corn syrup, milk, and salt. Stir well. Add oats, flour, and vanilla. Drop by scant teaspoonfuls of batter onto baking sheets, spacing cookies at least 3 inches apart. Cookies will spread a great deal. Bake at 375 degrees for about 6 minutes. Carefully remove from baking sheet while still slightly warm. The cookie will stiffen as it cools. If cookie gets too brittle to remove from baking sheet, return to oven for a few minutes. Grease cookie sheet again before baking another batch. Makes 48 cookies.

Pecan Bars

These pecan bar cookies are easy to make and always get rave reviews. What a treasure I found when I got this recipe from a "little old Italian lady" from New Orleans who did not want credit!

1/2 cup butter, room temperature
1 cup brown sugar
1/4 tsp. salt
2 cups all-purpose flour
2 1/2 cups pecan halves

Cream butter, sugar, and salt with an electric mixer for about 5 minutes. Add flour and continue beating for an additional 2 minutes.

Mixture will be crumbly. Shape dough into a ball. Using your fingers, press onto the bottom of a 9-inch by 13-inch pan. Place pecans side by side, covering the entire layer of dough.

Topping
1½ sticks (¾ cup) butter
⅓ cup brown sugar

Melt butter in a small skillet. Add brown sugar and stir well. Bring mixture to a boil. Boil for only 30 seconds—do not boil for a longer length of time. Pour mixture over pecans. Bake at 350 degrees for 22 minutes. Cool and refrigerate for at least 1 hour before serving. Cut into 32 bars with a serrated-edged knife. Makes 32 bars.

Rice Cakes

(*Frittele di Risa*)

This recipe was sent to me by my friend, Jean Donadio, who lives in Los Angeles. She got it from her sister-in-law, Frances Siliani, who once lived in Italy. Thirty years ago, when Jean sent the recipe, Frances lived in Caldine with her husband, Renato, and children, Simone, Sara, and Olimpia. There, St. Joseph's Day is a national holiday, and these cakes are eaten during the day's celebration.

½ cup rice
1¼ cups milk
1 tsp. butter
⅛ tsp. salt
1 tbsp. sugar
1 tsp. grated lemon peel
1 tbsp. rum
3 eggs, separated
½ cup flour
Oil for frying

Cook rice with milk, butter, salt, sugar, lemon peel, and rum. Add egg yolks and flour. Mix and place in refrigerator for 2 hours. When ready to fry rice batter, beat egg whites to a stiff meringue and fold into batter. Drop by spoonfuls into hot oil. Cook to golden brown. Drain then sprinkle with powdered sugar. Makes 12 rice cakes or sfingi.

Rice Sfingi

This rice "fingee" recipe came from Sarah Migliore of Good Hope via Gail Bosco of Luling. Mrs. Jack Cali of LaPlace makes a similar sfingi or fritelli but sweetens the batter with condensed milk.

2 cups short-grain rice
4 cups water
1 cup milk
1 cup sugar
1 tbsp. vanilla
1 tsp. cinnamon
2 cups flour
Oil for frying

Place rice and water in a pot over high heat. When water comes to a boil, cover pot and reduce heat. Mix cooked rice with milk. Add sugar, vanilla, cinnamon, and flour. Mix to make dough. Pat dough on a floured surface to 1/4-inch thickness then cut into finger-sized pieces. Fry in hot oil until nicely browned. Remove from oil and drain. Sprinkle with powdered sugar. Makes 50 pieces.

Yeast-Raised Sfingi

This recipe is from Mrs. Albert Culmone. She said that when she was growing up, the family did not have a car. Her dad would get up early in the morning and walk several miles to work.

1 package yeast
1 tsp. sugar
1 cup lukewarm milk
1 tsp. baking powder
1 egg
2 cups flour
1/2 tsp. vanilla
Oil for frying

In a medium-sized bowl, mix yeast with sugar and lukewarm milk. Let stand for 10 minutes so that yeast can dissolve. Add remaining ingredients and beat well. Cover and keep mixture warm. Let sit 15 minutes. Drop small pieces of dough into hot oil. Fry until golden brown. Remove from oil and drain. Sprinkle with powdered sugar. Makes 24 pieces.

St. Joseph Sfingi

Mrs. Joe Zito said that you cannot have a St. Joseph altar without the renowned sfingi. Some say that sfingi should be rolled in powdered sugar; others claim that the only way to serve these pastries is with granulated sugar.

8 eggs
¾ cup sugar
1 tbsp. vanilla
8 cups flour
10 tsp. baking powder
Oil for frying
Sugar, powdered or granulated

Beat eggs and sugar together until light. Add vanilla. Sift flour and baking powder together. Gradually add to egg mixture. Mix well. Drop by teaspoons in hot oil. Fry until light brown then remove and drain. Sprinkle with powdered or granulated sugar. Makes 8 dozen.

Italian Doughnuts

(*Sfingi*)

This recipe is from Rose Trenacosta of Brittany. Nutmeg is the preferred spice for these light fritters, called *sfingi*. The Zitos and the Marinos flavor their sfingi with vanilla and roll them in granulated sugar.

3 tsp. baking powder
2 cups flour
½ tsp. salt
⅓ cup sugar
1 tsp. nutmeg or other sweet spice
¼ cup oil
1 egg
¾ cup milk
Oil for frying
1 cup powdered sugar

Place all dry ingredients in a bowl. Beat oil, egg, and milk together. Stir into dry ingredients. Beat well. Drop by teaspoons into hot oil. Fry until golden. Remove from oil and drain. Sprinkle with powdered sugar. Makes 2 dozen.

Sfingi Dei San Giuseppe

These are better known as St. Joseph's Day cream puffs. The Noto and Distafani families shared this recipe.

1/2 cup butter
1/8 tsp. salt
1 cup water
1 cup all-purpose flour
4 eggs
1 tbsp. sugar
1/2 tsp. grated orange peel
1/2 tsp. grated lemon peel

Place butter, salt, and water in a 2-quart pot. Bring to a boil. Add flour and mix until dough no longer clings to the sides of the pot. Remove from heat and cool dough on a plate. Add 1 egg at a time until all eggs are incorporated into the dough. Beat in the remaining ingredients. Place dough in a pastry bag and squeeze 12 puffs of dough onto a greased cookie sheet. Bake at 400 degrees for 10 minutes then lower temperature to 375 degrees. Continue baking for about 50 minutes or until puffs are browned and crisp.

Cream Filling
3 tbsp. sugar
3 tbsp. flour
1/2 tsp. grated lemon rind
1/2 tsp. vanilla
2 cups milk
1 tbsp. butter
1/8 tsp. salt

Whisk all ingredients together in a heavy saucepan. Heat on low until cream is thick, stirring constantly. Cook for 4 minutes then cool. Using a pastry bag, fill sfingi with cream. Makes 12 sfingi.

St. Joseph Altar Glossary and Information Guide

Altar A display of various foods in veneration of St. Joseph. The Italian ladies with whom I spoke did not agree on the proper number of levels to an altar. Some said three levels; many approved of five. However, they did agree that all altars are different and can have as many levels as the builder desires. The altar can be built with wooden planks, like building steps, or by using a number of sturdy cardboard boxes. I have built the base of my altars both ways. When I assisted the ladies from Mary's Helpers with their altar at Louis Sais' property in Houma, Louisiana, we used empty Mam Papaul dinner-mix cases. They were eight inches by sixteen inches and provided the right height to accommodate the size of the breads and cuccidati on display. The exhibition of the food should be completed by a colorful tablecloth and background. First the altar should be covered entirely with inexpensive cloth, such as white sheets, cotton yardage, or similar material. Spread a decorative cloth over this material. Red is known as St. Joseph's color and is frequently the chosen background color.

Food of all kinds abound on the altars.

Anise Fresh anise, called *finnochi* in Italian, is always found on the altar (if the freeze didn't kill it all).

Baccala Dried codfish is a must on the altar. A smelly fish, it must be soaked before frying. Some say that seven kinds of fish should be placed on the altar, though no special kinds are named.

Bread Large Italian breads are made especially for the altar by Italian bakeries. The bread may be made in many shapes, but the wreath is the most popular. Small pieces of dough are placed on the wreath in the forms of a ball for Jesus, a crown for Mary, and a palm for St. Joseph.

Biscotti Refers to any Italian cookie.

Candles Candles, preferably large ones, are used on the altar and on tables extending from the altar. There, anyone wanting to make a donation to light a candle and pray may do so. Small baskets are placed near the candles to hold donations, which are given to the poor or a worthy cause. Nothing except St. Joseph candles are offered for sale at the altars.

Candy Candied almonds, licorice, and fudge of all kinds are used on the altar.

Cannoli Delicious, sumptuous, and sinfully full of calories, these pastries are a must on the altar. Make your own or buy them from Brocato's in New Orleans.

Cookies Platters and bowls of cookies of all kinds are placed on the tables extending from the altar. Be sure to have sesame, or "seed," cookies.

Cuccidati Large fig cakes made in various shapes such as the chalice, cross, monstrance, St. Joseph's sandals, and St. Joseph's staff. Use aspic cutters to make the decorative cutouts on the pastry.

Fava Beans These lucky beans, which look like large lima beans, are placed on the altar and given to everyone who attends the celebration. Buy the beans at Central Grocery on Decatur Street in the French Quarter. Bake beans at a low temperature, between 200 and 250 degrees, until they dry out and turn dark.

Fish A very large baked redfish is always found on the altar. The altar should also feature all types of seafood. I usually have a large platter with a few boiled shrimp, oysters, boiled crabs, etc. Lobsters are usually placed on a separate platter.

Flowers Flowers, as well as two of each type of vegetable and fruit, should adorn the altar. Use red lilies known as St. Joseph's lilies.

Hospitality Some say the outside of the home should be decorated with palmetto or olive branches to indicate hospitality. In rural areas celebrants fire a rifle to indicate that the St. Joseph dinner is being served to the public.

Lamb Cakes St. Joseph is often pictured with lambs, which the ladies say are Jesus' lambs. Molds for lamb cakes can be bought at

Notice the intricate designs of the cuccidati, large edible and decorative fig cakes. No two recipes quite duplicate each other, and each family thinks their recipe is the best.

most places that sell cake-decorating supplies or can likely be borrowed from someone in your neighborhood. Use a pound-cake recipe for an easy-to-handle cake. Decorate with white icing and coconut. Use raisins for the eyes and place a little ribbon around the lamb's neck.

Mudrica Toasted breadcrumbs sweetened with a little powdered sugar. The breadcrumbs are used to sprinkle over spaghetti and sauce in place of the usual grated cheese.

Pasta Uncooked dried pasta of all shapes and sizes. A platter of cooked pasta with the special Milanese sauce is among the food offerings because no meat is used on the altar.

Pinulatas Fried egg and flour dough, which is covered with caramelized sugar and shaped like a cone. Make large pinulatas for your altar and serve small pieces with cookies.

Rosary Cake A rosary cake is always found on the altar. Many people use cupcakes or biscotti (round cookies) placed on a platter in the form of a rosary.

Setting A table is set, usually in front of the altar, for the "Holy Family." Children take the parts of Jesus, Mary, and Joseph and sometimes other children are chosen to represent saints and angels. Dramatizing the "finding of lodging" story, the children come as a group to the door, knock, state their request, and are invited into the home. They are served orange appetizers then a very small amount of all foods on the altar.

Sfingi Used to describe various types of fried dough or cream puffs.

Statues Statues and pictures of St. Joseph are used on the altar. A large picture or statue is usually centered on the altar.

Vegetables Vegetable dishes of all kinds are usually placed at the lower level of the altar. Stuffed artichokes, fried vegetables of all kinds, and *frosia*, or vegetable omelets, should be placed where they can be reached and served. Try to keep perishables at the lower level so they can be removed easily and used yet not disturb the beauty of the altar.

Wine Usually sweet red wine is placed in decorative decanters on the altar.

Note: Many of the spellings for the dishes throughout this book are phonetic. These spellings were passed down from my interview subjects, and some are based on the Anglicized version of their original Italian names.

Helpful Hints

Many Italian cookie recipes do not call for salt, but this is not an error in the recipe. Salt brings out the flavor in food. If you choose to add salt, use 1/4 teaspoon for each cup of flour.

Use all-purpose flour in cookie recipes and bread flour for all breads.

Generally cookie yields are based on the weight of dried ingredients. Figure 10 to 12 cookies per cup of flour but bear in mind that the yield is dependent on the size of cookie you make.

Table of Measurements

2 cups equals 1 pint
2 pints equals 1 quart
4 tablespoons equals 1/4 cup
16 tablespoons equals 1 cup
1 stick of butter equals 1/2 cup
1 medium lemon yields 1 to 2 tablespoons grated rind
4 cups of flour equals 1 pound
2 cups of granulated sugar equals 1 pound
2 cups of rice equals 1 pound
3 1/3 cups powdered sugar equals 1 pound
4 cups shelled pecans or almonds equals 1 pound

Bibliography

Baiamonte, John V., Jr. "A Study of the Italians of Tangipahoa Parish, Louisiana." Ph.D. diss., Mississippi State University, 1972.

Dore, Granzia. "Some Social and Historical Aspects of Emigrations to America." *Journal of Social History* 2, no. 2 (1968): 110-20.

Magnaghi, Russell M. "Louisiana's Italian Immigrants Prior to 1870." *Louisiana History* 27, no. 1 (1986).

Randazzo, Lydia K. "From Can to Can't: The Story of Italian Immigration to Tangipahoa Parish." *Southeast Historical Association Paper* 7 (1980).

Saxon, Lyle, Edward Dreyer, and Robert Tallant, comp. *Gumbo Ya-Ya,* Gretna, LA: Pelican Publishing, 1987.

Scarpaci, Jean Ann. "Immigrants in the New South: Italians in Louisiana's Sugar Parishes 1880-1910." *Labor History* 16 (spring 1975): 165-83.

INDEX